TEACHING MO BIKE SKILLS

The Skills Training Manual for NICA Coaches

National Interscholastic Cycling Association

Lee McCormack : Race Line Publishing

For more information on mountain bike setup and riding and racing techniques, check out the book *Mastering Mountain Bike Skills 2nd Edition*

To learn all about BMX riding and racing, check out the book *Pro BMX Skills.*

ISBN 10 : 0-9745660-3-9   ISBN 13: 978-0-9745660-3-0

About this book

This National Interscholastic Cycling Association's skills training manual is based on NICA's experience working with high school mountain bike riders and the author's experience as a riding technique expert working with riders of all types and levels.

This book is an addendum to the NICA coaching manual, "Starting, Managing, and Coaching a High School Mountain Bike Team."

Some of this book is written directly to you, the coach. Much of this draft is written for "you" from a rider's perpective. We of course want our coaches to ride better, but when we say "you" we mean the rider. It's your job as the coach to help your riders understand this material from their perspective.

We encourage feedback on this manual and ask that you consider what other skills should be taught and/or referenced herein.

About the author

Lee McCormack is NICA's skills development director. He is a world renowned riding technique instructor. He uses his sequential teaching curriculum to help riders of all styles and levels — BMX, mountain and road; beginners to pros — ride better, safer and faster. Lee wrote and illustrated the books Mastering Mountain Bike Skills, Welcome to Pump Track Nation and Pro BMX Skills.

Lee has won numerous writing and informational graphics awards, and he was part of the team that won the 1998 Pulitzer Prize for public service. Lee lives in Boulder, CO, with his wife Arlette and their four kids — Kate (22), Ian (19), Fiona (2) and Finley (2). He rides as much as he can.

Check out his Lee's site: www.leelikesbikes.com.

Lee thanks NICA for their support. OK, let's ride!

Lee thanks NICA and his supporters:

Specialized Bicycle Components

Fox Racing Shox

Hayes Disc Brake

Sun Ringle

Answer Products

Gamut USA

Disclaimer

Mountain bike riding is potentially dangerous. NICA, the author and their representatives assume no liability whatsoever for any damages associated in any way with the information contained herein.

CONTENTS

1

BE A
GREAT COACH

Goals:

- Understand the roles and requirements of a high school mountain bike coach.

- Maintain a positive learning environment.

- Teach people the way they learn.

- Promote safety through skills instruction.

- Choose smart practice venues.

- Teach in an integrated way.

- Master the curriculum.

BEING A JUNIOR DEVELOPMENT COACH

Working with young athletes is a privilege and a responsibility. This section gives you some basic advice for how to conduct yourself as a coach.

For more details, see NICA's coach training manual, "Starting and Managing, and Coaching a High School Mountain Bike Team."

Developing your coaching philosophy

The way you approach your coaching is the product of myriad factors including your personality, training, experience, passion, the attributes of your athletes and — perhaps most importantly — your concern for your athletes.

Every coach is different, but every coach must consider these factors:

Be yourself. When you coach, you are still you. You're just you as a coach. To be anything else will deny your team your true awesomeness.

Be fair. Always.

Rewarding the process, not the outcome. This is crucial in a sport where only one rider in a class of 30 or more "wins."

Treating riders with equal respect and attention, no matter their skill level, personality, favorite bike brand, etc.

Finding a healthy balance between pushing your riders to improve and honoring them where they are. This is different for every athlete.

An effective coach connects with every rider.

NICA photo

Big Life Lessons. Bikes are amazing on their own, but being a mountain biker can help young athletes in many ways: teaching life skills, improving self-esteem, building strong friendships, living healthy lifestyles and more. If you run your program with passion and integrity, you won't have to teach these skills; they will seep in naturally.

What works? Pay attention to your athletes (as opposed to yourself). What helps them thrive? Do more of that.

Your roles as a coach

Being a NICA coach involves more than wearing short shorts and blowing a whistle. Some of your tasks include, but are not limited to:

Risk manager. This is the A-1 priority. Keep your athletes safe. For more info, familiarize yourself with NICA's risk management policies and guidance.

Role model. Everything you do is being watched and emulated. When you are with your team, make sure you behave professionally, use appropriate language and basically model the behavior you want out of your athletes.

Motivator. This is one job where just being STOKED is a job requirement. Be stoked no matter what (you are on bikes, remember?). Cheer everyone with enthusiasm and specificity. Celebrate every victory, from a race win to a well-executed cornering drill.

Organizer. No matter what you are doing, have a plan. Keep records. Be consistent. Delegate. If you can't handle some organizational duties, give them to someone who can.

Authority figure. You might be a mountain bike nerd, but you are in charge. When you have to, assert yourself in a strong, respectful and positive way. Set clear rules and expectations. Follow through with consequences.

What your riders need from you

These touch on what we've already said, but they are worth repeating. Your riders need:

Leadership. You are in charge. Wear that hat like it fits, and your riders will respect you.

Structure. Teenagers need parameters to follow. Practice is more effective with a plan.

Compassion. Support your riders in all areas. Be concerned for them, but never lower your expectations.

Praise. Even surly teenagers want to be told they did a great job.

Discipline. Remember rule A-1? Safety first. Riders respect coaches who create a safe, positive environment for them to rip on bikes.

Respect. While your student athletes are young and new to the sport, treat them with respect for who they are and the efforts they are making to succeed.

*What does that mean, anyway? It's all relative.

Whether you are a great mountain biker* means little to NICA or your athletes. What does matter: that you are a great coach and skills instructor. By using this curriculum to improve your riders' skills, you will make them healthier, happier and more successful — and you'll probably get pretty good yourself.

A whole lot of technical knowledge, people skills, experience and passion goes into becoming a great mountain bike teacher. Here are some of the big pieces:

MAINTAIN A POSITIVE LEARNING ENVIRONMENT

Don't push too hard. Never, ever, EVER coerce a rider into doing something s/he doesn't feel ready for. Once a rider feels stress, the body and mind tighten up, and good riding is almost impossible. At best, the rider struggles through the section and reinforces bad habits. At worst, the rider gets hurt. It's your job to take your riders, step by logical/exciting/satisfying step, to where they want to go.

Avoid bad stress. The excitement your riders feel before a race is good stress. Anxiety about failing or crashing or getting hurt is bad stress. Once riders experience bad stress, it becomes very difficult to learn and have fun. It's your job to keep your riders in a positive frame of mind. It's OK to feel some tingles; we just don't want the riders' emotions tipping toward panic.

A careful skills progression and an encouraging environment help riders do their best (and have fun).

NICA photo

It's OK to "fail." Fail is in quotes because when a rider tries something new and doesn't get it perfectly, it's not a failure. It's a chance to learn, improve, have more fun. Celebrate the process — the trying, learning and re-trying — rather than the outcome.

Give generous, specific praise. Tell riders exactly what they're doing well. (Also tell them exactly what they can do better.)

Be stoked! Your enthusiasm for riding and learning will become contagious and encourage the team riders to want to learn and excel!

TEACH PEOPLE THE WAY THEY LEARN

It's not important how you understand or learn riding skills. What's important: that you can consistently help your riders learn riding skills.

There are three basic types of learners:

1. **Auditory learners** – Listen to you explaining a skill.

2. **Visual learners** – Watch you demonstrate a skill.

3. **Kinesthetic/tactile learners** – Practicing and feeling the skill.

Most people have a dominant learning style, but they can learn in the other styles as well. When you teach a group, you must teach to all styles. Here's a good basic process for each lesson:

1. Explain. Tell riders what the skill is, when they'll use it and why they'll use it (extending inside arm into turn, every time they initiate a turn, to place the bike on edge and generate cornering force). Also explain the key dynamics (staying balanced on your feet, getting low, setting angle, letting steering column adjust per the bike's geometry, camber thrust). Start a dialog. Answer questions.

2. Demonstrate. As clearly, and perfectly, as you can, show the riders how to execute the skill. Talk as you ride. Call out important details as they happen. Show the skill from all useful angles (often from the front and side). Answer questions.

3. Practice. Set up a safe, controlled practice area and encourage riders to perform the skill themselves. Call out great examples. Repectfully offer constructive advice.

Also keep in mind:

Mix it up. The best lessons don't always go 1, 2, 3: Explain, Demonstrate, Practice. When Lee teaches his clinics, he dives in and out these modes as the group catches on, runs into blocks, catches on again, etc. Explain, demonstrate and practice as many times as it takes. When you teach bike skills, you are encountering habits, limitations related to riders' bodies and minds. Everyone learns differently. Keep addressing the issues in different ways until everyone has their a-hah moments.

Be extremely specific. All of the bike skills in this manual are comprised of sub-skills. Teach, practice and refine one sub-skill at a time (example: extending the inside arm to initiate a turn). Tell riders specifically what they are doing well and what they need to work on. As those movements become more integrated, practice the whole skill (railing a sweeping corner). Riders who struggle with details sometimes get it when everything is put together into a cohesive whole.

Be super-extremely specific. If a rider isn't getting the lesson, dive all the way down to individual body parts. In the case of extending the inside arm into a turn, focus on the elbow. Make sure it's bent 90 degrees before the turn, it's straight in the turn.

The more your riders talk to you

The better you can help them refine their position, technique and approach.

Encourage riders to talk about what they are feeling on the trail. This will benefit everyone on the team.

Ask questions and listen. Help riders learn to clearly express what they are experiencing and what they are challenged by while riding.

One thing at a time. Riders can only learn one new element at a time. Do not bury riders in a storm of details. Focus on one aspect of one sub-skill at a time. When your riders get it, move on.

How will we use this? Always drive home the point that this is a real skill the riders will use in real situations. Ask questions like, "Have you ever tried to start a turn, but the bike just wanted to go straight?" Then something like, "You probably weren't leaning your bike enough. Every turn has to start with the lean. That's how the bike is made to work. …"

Ask the riders. How do you feel? What do you notice? What do you think would happen if …? What did you learn? Where will you use this knowledge? This is called teaching by inquiry. Rather than shoving answers at riders, ask them questions that encourage them to provide their own answers. Most people — especially teenagers — would rather make their own decisions than be told what to think.

Have fun!

Get the brain out of the way.

Some athletes pay too much attention to the details, and that prevents them from learning the integrated movement. Instruct these riders to watch you perform a skill. Tell them not to think about what they see. Tell them to feel what they see. Rather than make comments to themselves, they should imagine what it feels like to perform the skill. They should feel your movement, your timing, the flow of the move. After you finish demonstrating, don't say a word. Have the rider get out there and rock the skill (You have to explain this before you demonstrate.). It's amazing how often this helps riders break through blocks.

PROMOTE SAFETY THROUGH SKILLS INSTRUCTION

Most mountain bike injuries are preventable. As a NICA coach it is critical that you do all you can to minimize risk and avoid overly dangerous situations. Consider the following essential concepts which will help minimize risk to your riders:

Appropriate terrain and group intensity level. Don't ride overly steep or technical trails. Don't let the group goad each other into taking big risks.

Pertinent skills. Make sure riders have the skills and instincts to handle their bikes in the terrain you will encounter. This includes knowing what to do if they lose control. If skills are not up to the terrain requirements, either change terrain or have riders walk the section (Heck, running with a bike is an important racing skill.).

Experience. The more time riders spend executing good skills in real situations, the more likely they will handle themselves correctly when things get hairy.

Adequate fitness. Fatigue makes riders sloppy and prone to mistakes.

Sound judgment. Both yours and the rider's. If a rider can't visualize a move, s/he should not try it. Do not cultivate a culture of "Go For It: It'll Be Fine." It might not be fine. Instead, teach your riders to recognize their current fitness, skills, experience, fatigue level and mood — and to ride within themselves.

Also:

Don't skip steps. Every advanced mountain bike skill — dropping, jumping, steep switchbacks — is comprised of the core skills explained in this manual. If a core skill is skipped or not mastered, the advanced skills will be compromised.

Start small. Before riders try 18-inch ledges, make sure they can ride off 6-inch curbs perfectly, then 12-inch curbs. Do not step it up until the current level is mastered.

Skill first, speed later. Start slow. Learn great skills. The speed will come naturally.

Practice perfection. Every rider has his/her own style, and that's great, but the fundamental skills are universal. In practice, make sure the core dynamics are perfect — and consistent. That's the only way for rider and coach to be confident when applying the skill on real terrain.

Let it go. When you're practicing, make perfection your mission. When you're racing or practicing race conditions, let it all go and find your flow. This is where all the hard work pays off. It's also really, really fun.

Timing is important. Don't try new skills at the end of practice when riders might be tired and more prone to crashing.

Have fun. Have we said that lately?

Skills are for everyone

Experienced riders might balk at the core skills in this manual, but experience has proven that expert riders usually get even more out of these lessons than beginners.

Why?

Expert riders often have:

1) bad habits that hold them back,

2) a commitment to the sport, and

3) the awareness to quickly learn and integrate the skills into their new, improved riding styles.

Beginning riders get a great start. They learn extra quickly because they don't have bad habits. They skip the whole trial-and-error process than most experienced riders have to endure.

Before you teach safe riding, it helps to master safe riding. Lee teaches the basics at a NorCal Leaders' Summit.

NICA photo

Trail Etiquette & Code of Conduct

Early in the season, coaches and riders should review NICA's "Trail Etiquette & Code of Conduct" document. All participants are required to sign this at beginning of season.

CHOOSE SMART PRACTICE VENUES

Where and when you practice determines your riders' experiences. Guidelines:

Sterile. When you first teach new skills, find the cleanest, plainest, least distracting area you can. You want riders to focus on the exact skill of the moment, not staying alive or being distracted by others. Parking lots and open fields are great for position, braking and cornering drills. If you want to teach pump, teach it on a pump track or BMX track before you take it to the rocks.

Not scary. If anyone in your group is afraid of the terrain, you are creating a negative experience. Bring the group to places everyone can feel confident. If more advanced riders act bored, encourage them to fine-tune their skills, try alternate lines or just plain go faster. It's amazing how interesting "boring" trails get at race pace.

> **Besides:** Most races are held on relatively tame terrain. Carrying good speed on green trails is more important to a racer than going big on the blacks.

Enough space. You need enough space to accommodate all your riders without trampling sensitive areas. This is especially important if you will be sessioning sections (which we recommend). Avoid busy times or popular hiking or dog walking areas.

Good sight lines. You should be able to see your riders over great distances.

> **Know your way.** Do not lead — or, worse, let your riders lead — the group into unknown terrain. Practice in known spots. If you decide to ride in a new place, pre-ride the area and come up with a teaching plan before everyone reaches the trail head.

Suggested venues

Cross country trails. These are the hallmark of mountain biking and represent the type of terrain on which your athletes will be racing. Whenever possible, ride trail. Follow IMBA's Rules of the Trail.

Roads. There are few better places to improve spin and focus on your pedalling fitness. Excellent when trails are too wet to ride. Follow traffic rules. Ride the road like you are mountain bikers. All skills still apply.

BMX tracks and pump tracks. Excellent places to build skills, fitness and team rapport. Discourage airtime. Encourage pumptime!

Parking lots and open fields. You can do a whole lot with just an open area. Refine position, brake as hard as you can, rip a makeshift slalom.

Be creative. You don't need a mountain to mountain bike.

Rules of the Trail

These commandments come from our friends at IMBA:

1. Ride open trails

2. Leave no trace

3. Control your bicycle

4. Yield appropriately

5. Never scare animals

6. Plan ahead

7. Wear a helmet whenever on a bike

http://www.imba.com/about/rules-trail

TEACH IN AN INTEGRATED WAY

Your ability to ride a mountain bike with safety, comfort and flair can be compared to a table with three legs. Your table is only as tall and strong as all three legs:

1. Skills

Skills let you do more on your bike, and do it better. Learn to pedal smoothly, lunge up ledges, carve corners and porpoise through the rocks. The bulk of this manual covers skills.

2. Fitness

Fitness lets you execute your skills faster, harder and longer. A good training program is as varied as the terrain we ride. It addresses mobility, strength, power, power endurance and long-term endurance. Fitness training is covered in Chapter 9 of "Starting, Managing, and Coaching a High School Mountain Bike Team."

3. Confidence

Mental training lets you make the most of your technical and physical abilities. You'll be focused enough to get a great start, resilient enough to hammer that entire climb and confident enough to flow down a technical descent.

Keep in mind:

Develop all three areas together. So many riders focus on fitness, and they think skills and confidence are functions of bravery. In fact, all three elements can be taught, learned and practiced — and each rider is only as strong as his or her weakest area. Build tall, stong tables!

These elements relate closely to each other.

- The more fit you are, the more effectively you can practice skills.

- The more skilled you are, the more terrain you can ride, which helps make you more fit.

- The more fit and skilled you are, the more positive experiences you have on the bike, and the more confident you become.

Always work all three legs. Whenever possible, try to simultaneously hone skill, develop fitness and enhance confidence. Ride with intentional focus, and celebrate the small victories.

The fourth leg would be equipment. Your bike, clothes and protective gear don't have to be fancy, but they have to fit properly and be well adjusted.

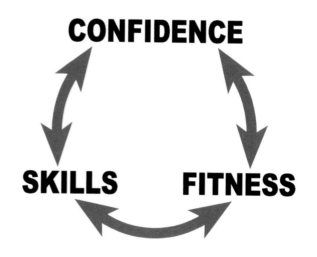

MASTER THE CURRICULM

You don't have to be crazy-fast or crazy at all. Just make sure you can demonstrate clean basic technique, and that you know enough to help riders to achieve that perfection.

If your riders need instruction you can't provide, consider bringing a more advanced rider into your program as an assistant coach.

The overall mission

The following skills curriculum is based on the writings and teachings of author/coach/rider Lee McCormack. Much of the content is inspired by Lee's books Mastering Mountain Bike Skills and Pro BMX Skills. The rest comes from his experience teaching riders of all styles and levels how to ride better.

This curriculum is based on a few simple notions:

1. Make sure the bike and rider fit each other.

2. Teach the rider how to be centered and balanced on the bike, then teach the rider how to use the entire cockpit. The more balanced and mobile the rider, the better the riding.

3. Teach the core skills —pedaling, braking, cornering, riding up and down stuff, and pumping terrain. Teach these with a keen awareness of 1) balance, 2) range of motion and 3) power. In that order.

4. Encourage riders to hone these core skills (true mastery comes from the basics), then expose them to situations where they can mix and match these skills in more advanced ways. Everything your athletes will ever want to do on a bike stems from the essential skills in this manual and the leadership your coaching provides.

5. Have fun!

And remember:

Practice does not necessarily make perfect.

Perfect practice makes perfect.

2

FIT BIKES TO RIDERS

Goals:

- Encourage riders to wear appropriate gear
- Encourage riders to select appropriate bikes
- Position saddle for safe, efficient pedaling.
- Position handlebar for comfort and control.
- Position brake levers for easy, powerful speed control.
- Adjust suspension correctly.
- Encourage riders to take care of their bikes.

WEAR THE RIGHT GEAR

As a coach, encourage your riders to wear the right stuff.

Helmets. Always. Any time they are on a bike. Helmets should fit correctly, be in good condition and meet current safety standards. Any new cycling-specific helmet from a reputable manufacturer will be safe (but it must be worn, and worn correctly!). Check each rider's helmet to ensure a proper fit and that there are no cracks or other signs of wear.

Eyeglasses. Riders should cover their eyes on all rides. This improves vision and comfort, and it can prevent painful and possibly debilitating injuries. Even a slightly lacerated cornea, which typically heals fast, hurts like heck! (Ask Lee.)

Jerseys. It can be relaxing and "hardcore" to ride in a cotton t-shirt, but sweaty cotton stays sweaty and can make riders feel cold. Bike-specific jerseys are more comfortable and just plain work better on rides. Besides, you know your team has a sweet jersey.

Gloves. While some pro racers choose to ride without gloves, we suggest you encourage your riders to wear cycling gloves whenever they ride. Gloves improve control, and they prevent injuries. Even if a scraped-up palm is a minor injury, it really hurts, and it really gets in the way of everyday living.

Shorts. Some young riders will not feel comfortable wearing form-fitting Lycra shorts. That's OK, but encourage all of your riders to wear cycling-specific shorts with padded liners. Even if these shorts look baggy and casual, they are far safer and more comfortable than non-bike shorts and underwear.

Socks. Cycling-specific socks are thin, fit well in cycling shoes, wick away sweat and come in lots of cool colors and designs. Wet feet can lead to blisters; let's keep those feet dry.

Modern helmets are light, cool and comfortable. Photo from Specialized Bicycle Components

Shoes. Riders who use clip-in pedals must use cycling-specific shoes. Flat-pedal riders will appreciate the extra grip and protection they get from bike-specific shoes like those made by 5.10 and Teva. Skate shoes work well. Hiking and running shoes will do the job, as long as they have low tread that sticks to the pedals.

Arm and knee/leg warmers. These fit in jersey pockets and make chilly rides much more pleasant. One guideline: If it's under 65 degrees, cover your knees.

Vests and jackets. Make sure riders are prepared for any weather. Remember: A warm core makes a warm rider.

Protective padding. Knee and elbow pads add confidence and prevent injuries. While your riders might not want to race cross country in pads, encourage them to wear pads during practice and when they're trying new things.

PICK THE RIGHT BIKE

As the chart below shows, there are all kinds of mountain bikes for all kinds of riding. Most NICA rider/racers will be best served by the lower-left end of the spectrum: hardtails, cross-country race   bikes and cross-country trail bikes.

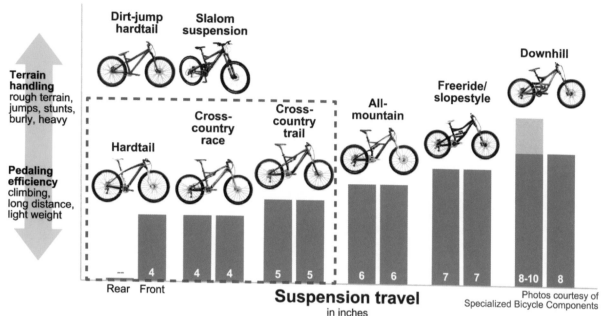

Photos courtesy of Specialized Bicycle Components

(These are the emerging "standards." There is still some variation among bike makers.)

Rear suspension adds control and speed in rough terrain, but it also adds weight and cost.

29-inch wheels make all mountain bikes — especially hardtails — roll more smoothly over rough terrain. For many riders, especially those just starting out, a 29er hardtail delivers the perfect blend of lightness, smoothness and affordability.

Smaller riders might feel better on smaller — and still trusty — 26-inch wheels.

Choose appropriate tires

While many high-level cross country racers ride tires with tiny knobs for fast rolling, all but the most expert riders should choose tires with big knobs. This gives them much more control in corners and in loose conditions.

Tire pressures should range from about 30-40 psi for inner tubes, as low as 25 psi for tubeless. Experiment to see what works best for you — then leave it alone.

Tiny knobs: Best for experts

Big knobs: Good for everyone

MEET YOUR NEW BEST FRIEND

Review these terms with your team members early in the season and make learning about equipment fun. Encourage a more seasoned student athlete to assist or lead a talk on proper bike set-up and maintenance.

Bikes are so cool. Here are the main components of a mountain bike. This will give you and your team a common understanding and language when talking bike parts.

Rim brakes
Some older bikes might have brakes that the rims instead of the rotors. Properly adjusted rim brakes have plenty of stopping power — especially when the rider has great braking technique.

PROPER BIKE FIT

The experts at the Boulder Center for Sports Medicine recommend that riders get fit by qualified professionals, and that coaches look for these general signs of a well-matched bike and rider. Individuals vary, but this is a good place to start.

1. **Extended leg is bent about 30 degrees** at full extension.

   Foot is level or pointed slightly down. If seat is too high, rider will point toes excessively while maintaining proper knee angle.

2. **Front of knee is above end of crank arm** when pedal is at 3 o'clock.

3. **90-degree angle between arm and torso** with elbows slightly bent.

If your riders look very different from this, reconsider their positions. For more details, check the Saddle and Handlebar sections (next pages).

The most common mistake is placing the bars too low and forward in attempt to achieve a low "racing" position. That position is not proven to improve pedaling performance, but it clearly impedes bike handling.

Strive for a neutral, comfortable position that offers good bike control. Speed comes from that.

Young riders' bones grow faster than their muscles, leaving their muscles too tight for low positions and long, "racy" cockpits. Young riders, especially boys, should generally have upright positions like the one shown.

If you need to lower your torso, say for a steep climb, you should simply bend your arms.

Three steps to a good fit

1. Pick the right bike size. Rider should have clearance when straddling the top tube. Most bike makers provide sizing guides.

2. Place the saddle in the right place for comfortable, efficient pedaling.

3. Place the handlebars for comfort and control.

High school aged athletes may experience dramatic growth spurts and, thus, it is critical that coaches monitor their riders closely. A well fitting bike at the beginning of a season may not suit the rider three months later!

About 90° between arm and torso

Bars around saddle height

Knee bent about 30°

90°

30°

Lester Pardoe, Boulder Center for Sports Medicine coaching specialist and biomechanical technician, demonstrates a neutral bike fit.

NEVER move the saddle from the optimal pedaling position to make a bike that's too long or short fit "better."

Use either measure

Saddle

The most common mistake, according to the experts at the Boulder Center for Sports Medicine, is setting the saddle too low and too far forward. This causes pain in the front of the knee. Some guidelines:

Fore-aft position

Traditionally speaking, with your pedal at 3 o'clock, the bone right below your knee should be directly above your pedal spindle. (Easier: The front of the knee should be above the end of the crank.) Among experienced riders and fitters, this isn't gospel, but it is dogma.

Seat farther forward means more quads and knees.
It tends to work better on climbs.

Seat farther backward means more hamstrings and hip flexors.
It tends to work better on descents.

Your best bet: Start with the traditional position then adjust from there.

Saddle level
for all-around riding

Saddle pointed down 5°
for extended climbing

Angle

A level saddle works well in most situations.

Nose pointed down feels better (because it feels level) on steep climbs and on suspension bikes whose rear ends sag under rider weight. For extended climbing, consider pointing your saddle down 1-5 degrees.

Nose pointed up feels better on steep descents.
Gravity and freestyle riders point their saddles up 10 degrees or more.

Your best bet: Start with the saddle level. If the nose often pokes you, tilt it down.

Height

Set saddle height so your knee is bent about 30 degrees when your leg is at full extension (at about 5:30 on the clock; see previous page). Most riders will feel good within a few degrees of this point.

Another quick check is the Italian foot drop. With butt on seat and both legs hanging down, the heel of the shoe should barely touch the pedal (at left).

Higher saddles make it easier to spin higher cadences. Once you go too high, your power output drops significantly. If the back of your knees hurt, your saddle might be too high.

Lower saddles give you more room to handle your bike. This is why many trail riders lower their seats for descents. If your knees hurt under the kneecaps, your saddle might be too low for safe pedaling. Climb at your ideal height; drop the seat for DH!

Handlebars

Once you position your saddle for optimal pedaling, it's time to position your bars (more precisely, your grips) to fit your body and riding style.

Start stock. Product managers spec their bikes with bars and stems that match the intended use of the bike and the likely size of the rider. For most riders, the stock setups work well.

It's all about riding style. These are actual relationships between saddles and bars on stock Specialized mountain bikes.

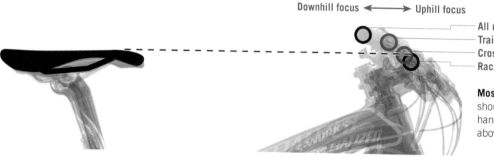

Downhill focus ⟵⟶ Uphill focus

All mountain - Enduro
Trail - Stumpjumper FSR
Cross country - Epic
Race - Stumpjumper HT

Most high school racers should start with their handlebars at or slightly above saddle height.

Long and low works. As the bars get farther from the saddle, they also get lower. If you lengthen the stem without also lowering the bars, the rider might feel like s/he has to reach extra far for the bars.

Short and high works. As the bars get closer to the saddle, they also get higher. If you shorten the stem without also raising the bars, the cockpit will feel cramped, especially while seated.

Quick check: When rider is seated with slightly bent arms, there should be about a 90-degree angle between the torso and upper arm.

When to change handlebar position

Look for these signs that stem length/rise or handlebar rise should be changed:

Rider is reaching for the bars. In the saddle, the angle between the torso and upper arm is much more than 90 degrees. Bars should be below saddle only in cases of very experienced and flexible riders.

Rider looks cramped. In the saddle, the angle between the torso and upper arm is much less than 90 degrees. If the cockpit is shortened, the bars should be well above the saddle.

Rider wants help in technical terrain. In this case, which is common with riders of all levels, move the bars backward and upward to a more downhill-focused position.

Handlebar width: the pushup test

Some of your riders will have handlebars that are too narrow or wide. Ask your riders to do some pushups. They will likely place their hands in their positions of maximum strength — and that's typically the perfect handlebar width.

Controls

Proper placement of your brake levers and shifters reduces strain and improves control. We are all about positioning the rider for easy, successful riding. Please check the control placement for all your riders.

Perfect brake lever adjustment on AA BMX Pro Jason Richardson's bike.

Brake levers

99 percent of riders have their brake levers set too far outboard and at the wrong angle and reach.

Side-to-side position: Move the lever toward the stem until the the index finger rests on the end of the lever. This is probably farther inboard than you expect, but it gives maximum braking power with minimal effort.

Angle: Set the angle so, when you are braking hard, there's a straight line through your forearm, hand, grip and lever. 45 degrees from horizontal is a good start.

Reach: Set the reach to the first knuckle of the index finger is on the end of the lever. Riders with smaller hands should move their levers toward their grips. Some benefit from women-specific bikes, which often have special levers for smaller hands.

MAKE SURE YOUR RIDERS' BRAKE LEVERS ARE SET CORRECTLY!
Also, check the condition of your rider's brake pads and brake mechanisms.

Shifters

Put your brake levers exactly where they need to be for easy, powerful braking. Once they are set, put your shifters where they fit.

If your shifters are inboard of your brake levers, the shifters might be hard to reach.

If your shifters are outboard of your brake levers, you might accidentally hit the shifters with your knuckles. You'll probably have to remove the shift indication windows.

Find the compromise that works for you. Remember: Perfect brake placement is critical. Perfect shifer placement is convenient.

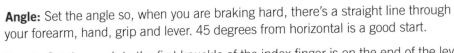

Brake lever is well inboard for maximum leverage. Straight line through forearm, hand, grip and lever. First knuckle on lever. Shifter moved outboard the brake lever. If you ride with a handlebar bell: Make sure it's positioned to allow safe use while riding.

Pedals

Your riders can choose from two styles of pedals: clip-in and flat. Pedals with toe clips and straps are not a good choice.

Flat pedals

The best flat pedals have pins or teeth that stick to soft-soled shoes.

Pros: They teach engaged pedaling, and they force the rider's feet to move with the terrain. Best way to learn pumping, hopping and other critical skills. Guarantee that rider is driving weight into the pedal spindles. Increased rider confidence in technical terrain.

Cons: If you're used to clips, they take time to learn. Harder to ride in very rough conditions. Reduced pedaling power for most riders.

Clip-in pedals

Clip-in pedals engage with a cleat mounted to the bottom of a stiff-soled shoe. Many clip-in pedals can be adjusted to provide for easier release, which is helpful while learning.

Pros: Increased pedaling power, especially when it's very rough or steep, from a dead stop and when the rider is fatigued. Increased control in bumpy terrain, because you're not worrying about your feet coming off the pedals.

Cons: They allow riders to develop poor riding habits, including: pulling with the feet when trying to hop, not driving weight into pedal spindles and riding in a generally stiff and undynamic manner.

Flat pedal (top)
and clip-in pedal.

Learn both: Flat pedals teach balance and flow that benefit every rider. We recommend that all riders become proficient on flat pedals — perhaps during the off season. Once riders learn to handle their bike well with both types of pedals, they should choose which works best for them.

Beginners should not be forced to clip in. Start with flat pedals. When you gain confidence, then consider clipping in.

Cranks

Cranks are expensive to change, but watch your smaller riders. If a rider is rocking his or her hips to bring the pedals up, the cranks might be way too long and need to be replaced with shorter ones.

* Because most cross country bikes use air springs, we don't cover sag adjustments for coil springs. Check the bike and suspension maker's web sites.

SUSPENSION BASICS

Properly tuned suspension makes a bike ride like a dream. Improperly tuned suspension makes it ride like a nightmare. In fact, no suspension is better than wrong suspension. Too bad almost all of your riders' suspension settings will be wrong.

For every rider and bike, take the time to get a basically good suspension setup. Go in this order:

1. Set sag

What it is: The most important suspension setting and our starting point. Sag is the amount your suspension compresses under your body weight. The more air pressure you have in an air fork or shock*, the less it sags. The less air pressure, the more it sags.

What it should do: Most cross country bikes should sag through about 25 percent of their available suspension travel (check your owner's manual). This holds the bike up at the proper height while letting the suspension extend into low spots.

How to set it: Put a small zip tie on your fork stanchion or an o-ring on the shaft of your rear air shock*. Push them down as far as they will go. This is a team effort:

- One person holds the bike upright by holding the rear wheel between the legs.

- The rider dons all riding gear, gets on the bike in the attack position, bounces up and down and lets the suspension settle.

The sag on this Specialized Stumpjumper is perfect. Note the locations of the o-ring (rear) and zip tie (front).

- A third person moves the zip tie and o-ring down so they touch the fork slider or shock canister.

- Rider gently gets off the bike, being sure not to compress the suspension.

- Measure the distance the zip tie and o-ring have moved from the starting bottom position. This is your sag. If the suspension sagged too much, add air and check again. If the suspension didn't sag enough, remove air and check again.

Read the manual! Many bike and suspension makers tell you with great accuracy how much air pressure to use for your body weight.

Tip: Make sure the front and rear ends have equal percentages of sag. Unequal sag means uneven balance, and that makes bikes handle poorly.

2. Set rebound damping

What it is: Hydraulic valving that controls the rebound of your fork or shock after it gets compressed. More rebound damping means slower rebound. Less rebound damping means faster rebound.

What it should do: It should let your suspension extend fast enough to meet the next bump, while slowing it down enough so it doesn't feel bouncy. This is a balance.

How to set it: Start with the bike maker's suggested setting for the amount of air pressure you are using. If the bike maker doesn't have a setup chart, check the web site of the suspension maker. These recommended settings are usually very good.

You adjust the rebound by turning the rebound dial. Clockwise usually slows the rebound. Counterclockwise usually speeds it up.

You want the suspension to rebound as quickly as possible without feeling bouncy. In general, the faster you ride, the faster you need your rebound.

One quick test: Dial the rebound to its fastest setting. Ride off a curb. You want the suspension to compress downward, rebound upward then stay up. If your suspension goes down, up then down again, it's bouncing — and that's not good. Increase rebound damping one click at a time until the bouncing stops.

Dialed suspension helps your body deal with impacts, but it is NOT a replacement for proper body position.

Yosei Ikeda photo

3. Set compression damping

What it is: Hydraulic valving that controls the compression of your fork or shock. Less compression damping makes it easier for your suspension to move through all its travel and "bottom out." More compression damping resists movement and uses less suspension travel. It also helps your bike ride higher.

What it should do: Coupled with the proper air pressure, your compression damping should make your bike feel firm when you're pedaling or pumping, yet absorb bumps and use all available travel without bottoming out harshly.

How to set it: LEAVE IT ALONE! Many forks and shocks don't have compression adjustments, which is good because it's easier to get them wrong than right. If your bike has adjustable compression, start in the stock position and don't change it unless you have a good reason.

Good reasons to change compression damping: First re-check your sag. If your suspension is moving too much, increase compression. If your suspension isn't moving enough, decrease compression. READ THE MANUAL!

What about ProPedal? The firmness of some shocks (and forks) can easily be switched to suit different riding conditions. Experiment to find your favorite setting.

Don't mess with it: Find a setting that feels good on your normal rides, then ride it everywhere.

Many of your riders' suspension systems may be in serious need of maintenance and/or have broken components (e.g., blown seals, leaking oil, etc.).

If you see significant dirt and oil accumulating down the fork leg, the fork might have a blown seal and need servicing.

Suspension troubleshooting

Most riders have no idea what their suspension is doing. At best they have a vague idea that the bike feels good or bad, but that's about the extend of the detail. Fact is, perfectly dialed suspension makes everything feel easier.

As a coach, especially in the beginning of the season, you should pay close attention to your riders's suspension. Ask riders what they are feeling. Watch how their bikes behave on various terrain. Shooting video and analyzing suspension behavior (and riding technique) can be a great team activity.

Problem: Bike bounces up and down after hitting bump or dropping off curb
Solution: Increase rebound damping.

Problem: Bike feels good over first bump but gets harsher over subsequent bumps.
Solution: Your fork or shock is "packing up" — getting more and more compressed — because it can't extend before it hits the next bump. Decrease rebound damping.

Problem: Excessive bottoming (even with correct sag); too much bouncing while pedaling.
Solution: Increase compression damping.

Problem: Bike feels harsh on big bumps, feels harsh or chatters on small bumps, has poor traction in corners, is not using full travel (even with correct sag).
Solution: Decrease compression damping.

When you're loading for a bunny hop, your suspension should compress at least half way.

If you're going to make adjustments, read this!

Before you start, write down your air pressures and dial settings.

Only use a functioning shock pump that's designed for your equipment. Don't mess with the setting if you don't have the right tool!

Adjust one thing at a time.

Adjust one click at a time.

Take the time to compare settings. Feel can be deceptive. Try riding sections with a timer.

Be methodical and patient!

When in doubt: Do exactly what the bike or suspension maker says to do.

CARING FOR YOUR BIKE

Mountain bikers rely on their bikes for fun and safety. Improperly maintained bikes are no fun, and they can be dangerous.

Regular maintenance

Make sure your riders:

Keep it clean. If your bike is dirty, clean it with hot water and soap. Use a sponge or soft cloth on the frame and suspension. Use a scrub brush for components and hard-to-reach areas. Use a different brush for your chain, chainrings and cassette.

Check all fasteners. If you ride your bike, the bolts will get loose. Start at the stem and work your way back to the rear brake. Don't be surprised if your suspension's pivot bolts need to be tightened. Teach your riders about proper torque.

Lube the chain. Clean it first. Apply a line of bike-specific chain lube along both sides of the roller. Spin the cranks to let the lube settle. Wipe off the excess with a rag or cloth (a worn-out t-shirt or dish towel are great).

Maintain proper tire pressure. What's the ideal pressure? That's a can of worms. For general trail riding, most high school riders using inner tubes should be in the 30- to 40-psi range. Tubeless tires can be run at lower pressures, down into the 20s. Experiment to find a good setting. Check it before every ride.

Replace worn out parts. This includes tires, brake pads, grips, chains, chainrings, cassettes and cleats. Inexpensive replacements tend to become expensive and potentially dangerous when you ignore them.

Mandatory trailside repairs

Make sure your riders can handle these emergency tasks. Practice ahead of time.

Flat tire. Every rider should carry enough parts and tools to manage two flat tires.

Quick derailleur adjustment. Everyone on the team should know how to use the barrel adjusters.

Broken chain. Not such an issue in these modern times, but riders must be able to handle broken links on the trail.

To sum it up:

Set your bike up for comfort and confident handling.

Take the time to make it right.

Once it feels good, LEAVE IT ALONE!

Encourage riders to keep cleaning equipment where they store their bikes. This will make regular cleaning more likely.

At each practice, set a good example by having a seasoned student athlete or yourself demonstrate and ensure that all participants "shake, rattle, and roll" their bikes to identify any mechanical issues. By quickly shaking and rolling the bike and checking the various systems, a rider should be able to identify any malfunctions or damaged parts that need to be addressed prior to riding.

TROUBLESHOOTING

Your riders will show up with whatever bikes they have, and in many cases there's not much you can do about that. However, by working closely with your riders and scheduling very early season "bike clinics," you can troubleshoot and rectify many mechanical and ill-fitting bike issues to ensure athletes are properly outfitted to safely ride.

Here are some essential things to look for:

Problem: You wouldn't feel confident riding one of your team members' bikes.

Solution: You're asking kids to ride trails with you. You must ensure their equipment is at least up to your standards. Work with the rider's family to discuss the situation and determine if they are able to secure another bike. If necessary, consider finding a loaner bike that is suitable for the rider.

Some teams have developed impressive quivers of loaner bikes and assorted gear through "Lycra drive" donation campaigns and the generosity of local cycling clubs and teams. Make friends and don't be afraid to ask for donations!

Problem: Riders' bikes make bad noises. Anything beyond the growl of tires, click of gears and clatter of chains is bad.

Solution: Make sure the noises get chased and fixed.

Fork parts

Steerer

Crown
Stanchion
Arch

Slider

Dropout

Problem: A rider with good form looks out of control on rough terrain.

Solutions: Double-check the suspension setup.

Problem: You hear suspension bottoming with a metal-to-metal noise.

Solutions: Double-check the suspension setup. You'll need more air pressure.

Problem: A rider with good form can't seem to lean the bike enough or stay balanced on steep downslopes.

Solution: The cockpit might be too long. Look into a shorter stem.

Shock parts

Reservoir

Preload
collar

Coil
spring

Problem: A rider's seat interferes with good form.

Solutions: It's possible to learn good form by moving around a high seat, but it's hard to do. Many riders learn faster when they practice proper movement with low seats. Once they get the movements, they can learn to move around high seats.

3

DIAL IN THEIR POSITION

Goals:

- Make sure riders master the neutral attack position.

- Teach and drill this position one body part at a time, starting with the feet and working up to the eyes.

- Encourage riders to expand their use of the entire cockpit.

- Develop and reinforce proper riding position and balance to strengthen bike handling skills.

THIS IS THE ATTACK POSITION

A neutral attack position places the rider in the middle of the bike's cockpit, balanced and ready for anything. Every riding skill starts and ends with a neutral attack position.

Here are the keys to that position:

Heavy feet, light hands!

This is the key to everything.

As long as your weight is driving into your feet, and your hands are neutral, your bike will handle well and you'll be as safe as possible.

And you'll be ready to quickly respond to different situations.

5. Shoulders low, blades down and back

4. Torso level

3. Hips back

8. Head up, eyes out

7. **Hands weightless**, wrists straight

6. Elbows out

2. Knees bent

1. **All weight on feet**, feet parallel with cranks

Efficiency and comfort: This position requires mobility, strength and endurance.

Riders should do what they must to stay comfortable on the bike. It's OK to sit down or stand up on straight/smooth sections, but:

When it's time to Ride with a capital R, get in your attack position!

Here are more details by body part. A good attack position starts at the feet. Start there and work your way up.

FEET

Everything starts with the feet! Whatever the net force is (gravity, braking, impact, any combination), it should drive directly into the pedal spindles — perpendicular to the cranks.

Keep feet parallel with cranks. The only exceptions are cornering with a foot down and pedaling. Keeping feet parallel with cranks keeps the rider's weight driving into the pedal spindles, rather than pushing forward or falling backward, which upset bike handling.

In general:

Flat ground: both feet and cranks are level.

Going downhill: cranks, feet and body rock backward.

Going uphill: cranks, feet and body rock forward.

Braking and/or hitting bumps: cranks, feet and body rock backward.

Uphill, constant speed

Feet and cranks level with horizon, body forward on bike.

Flat ground, constant speed

Feet and cranks level.

Pre-loading for a bunny hop
Rocking into manual and laying big force into rear wheel. Feet, cranks and body rotate back. Force perpendicular to cranks.

Downhill, braking

Feet parallel with cranks. Cranks and body rotated back.

Moving around high seat

KNEES

Always bent. Sometimes slightly. Never locked straight.

Straighten legs into low spots. Stand tall (heavy feet, light hands).

Bend legs over high spots. Crouch low (heavy feet, light hands!).

If the terrain moves up and down, your legs should move at least as much. You have to work the terrain plus your suspension.

The more range you can get from your legs, the faster, smoother and safer you are on big bumps.

Smooth rollers like this are ideal practice.

Yosei Ikeda photos

Keep your knees on the same plane, as if they share a pivot. This helps rider stay balanced over the pedals, and it improves power and efficiency. Rider is supporting and driving through both hips evenly, rather than favoring one side.

This is hard to make perfect all the time, but it's worth practicing (so it can eventually be perfect all the time).

HIPS

Most support and power should come from the hips. Few riders know how to use their hips effectively.

Feel your butt muscles. Most riders ride with their butts tucked forward. This emphasizes quads over glutes. To fully engage your hip muscles, push your hips back.

Push your hips back! This folds your torso level, which brings your shoulders down and gives you the arm range to handle big bumps and tight turns.

When the going gets crazy, you have to get your hips back. That's the only way to bring your shoulders low and give you the range you need.

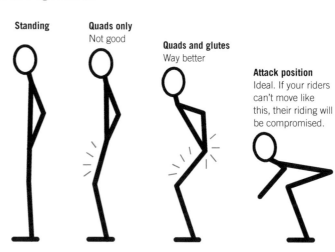

Standing

Quads only
Not good

Quads and glutes
Way better

Attack position
Ideal. If your riders can't move like this, their riding will be compromised.

The longer the cockpit, the more the rider must push the hips back to get the shoulders low enough for adequate arm range. Long/low stems *require* a long/low position. Shorter cokpits (with short/tall stems) let riders stand a bit more upright.

Improve mobility. If your riders can't access the positions shown on this page (and most can't, especially fast-growing boys), work on their mobility with off-the-bike strength and mobility exercises, including yoga.

Hips back, torso level, balanced on feet, arms very bent

Extend from the hips

Head and torso stay level. Sweet!

Yosei Ikeda photo

TORSO

The torso is, of course, tied to the hips. Doing good hip things helps you do good torso things.

Push your hips back! Don't think about bringing your shoulders down; that only pulls you too far forward. Push your hips back and let your torso fold flat. (See stick figures on previous page.)

Level. Strive to keep your back level with the horizon. You don't need to ride this low all the time; when it's time to Ride with a capital R, get down there.

Neutral. Back is neither hunched nor arched. Strive for a straight line through the hip and spine. Watch for young riders keeping their hips upright and bending forward at their waists. Riders should not look like scared cats when descending!

Get low! When the terrain gets steep, tight or unknown, get your torso as low as you can. This gives you the arm range to extend into holes, lean into corners or do whatever else you need to do to safely stay on your bike.

This MTB fun is brought to you by a level torso. This is the only way to ride these sections smoothly.

Yosei Ikeda photos

SHOULDERS

The shoulders are, of course, tied to the torso, which is tied to the hips. Doing good hip things helps you do good torso things, which helps you do good shoulder things.

Get them low. Remember, if you push your hips back and let your torso fold flat, your shoulders will be low.

No hunching forward. This is inefficient and weak on both the climbs and descents. Also, it does not look cool.

Manualling a roller: Pushing down with hips, anchoring with shoulders.

Down and back. Pull your shoulder blades down toward your hips. Keep your shoulder blades anchored to your back. Feel the pinch. Use (and develop) those back muscles.

Shoulders away from ears. That's a useful cue to help prevent riders from hunching their shoulders, especially when they're uncomfortable or afraid.

When your shoulders are hunched forward, you feel worthless and weak. When they're anchored down and back, you feel important and mighty. You're also stronger. Yosei Ikeda photos

ELBOWS

Bend your elbows. Sometimes slightly. Never locked straight.

Elbows out. Not only does this look cooler at every speed, it creates a stronger stucture, improves range and lets you express your awesome power.

90 degrees. When you're in your attack position, strive for an almost 90-degree bend. This puts you in the middle of your range of motion.

If the terrain moves up and down or side to side, your arms should move at least as much. You have to work the terrain plus your suspension.

Even while pushing into a transition, the elbows are OUT.

Watch your riders' elbows. Are they bending in the high spots and extending into the low spots? Great riding requires full range of motion.

Yosei Ikeda photos

HANDS

Light hands! As long as all your weight is in your feet — and your hands are weight-less — you are safe and your bike will roll properly. Challenge your riders to see how dainty they can be. Ride with Tea Party fingers.

Light hands. Heavy feet! Seriously.

Always check:

If you feel pressure on your palms, shift your weight back.

If you feel pulling on your fingers, shift your weight forward.

> **Light hands, heavy feet!**

Keep straight wrists. Adjust your grip to keep a straight line through your forearm, hand and grip. Below are three different situations.

Watch your riders' hands. Many will grip the bars and never move their hands. This leads to bent wrists, extra tension and general weakness.

When the terrain changes, change your grip:

Yosei Ikeda photos

Seated pedaling

Standing pedaling

Steep drop

HEAD AND EYES

Up and out. Keep your head up and your eyes out as far as possible. This helps maintain balance, makes it easier to pick effective reference points and provides you the longest sight line possible. Also, compared with drooping your head and staring at your front wheel, it looks less apologetic and more confident.

Head up and eyes out is critical to good riding, and it's the first thing everyone forgets, especially when they feel stressed.

Watch your riders' heads and eyes. Make sure heads are up and eyes are looking in good places. Good places to ride, not good places to crash.

While you're at it:

- Look through the next turn.

- Look through the next bumps.

- Practice visual reference points on your local trails and at race tracks.

- Listen for dogs barking, horses galloping and hikers talking. Always be attentive and on the lookout for other trail users.

For more details, check the Pick Smart Lines section.

It's too late to look at the turn or rock you're currently riding. You need to be looking at your *next* turn and rock.

Once you commit to a move, let your body take over.

If you are here ...

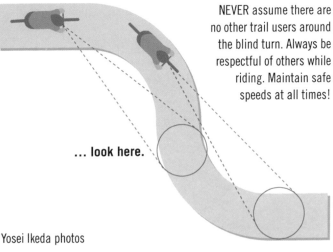

NEVER assume there are no other trail users around the blind turn. Always be respectful of others while riding. Maintain safe speeds at all times!

... look here.

Yosei Ikeda photos

ATTACK POSITION CHECKLIST

☐ **Heavy feet, light hands**

☐ **Feet** heavy and driving into pedals

☐ **Knees** bent and moving with terrain

☐ **Hips** back and powerful

☐ **Torso** level and straight

☐ **Shoulders** low with blades down and back

☐ **Elbows** out, bent and moving with terrain

☐ **Hands** light and wrists straight

☐ **Head, eyes and ears** up, out and attentive.

☐ Heavy feet, light hands!

WORK THAT RANGE OF MOTION

The attack position is the rider's base position: the average of all rider positions.

In order for riders to control their bikes on a wide range of terrain, they must develop complete, fluid access to their entire cockpits. Every mountain bike skill is a combination of these basic movements. Master these. Master the bike.

Practice these essential positions with your riders. These fun drills are ideal for early season rides in large grass fields or wherever riders are protected from cars and other hazards.

All the way up

Goal: Extend legs and arms fully and powerfully when appropriate (don't spend more than a moment like this).

Uses: Extending into low spots, pumping backsides, generating downforce for pumps, hops and jumps.

All the way down

Goal: Crouch low. If you're on a trail bike, get your shoulders down to the bars and your belly on the saddle. Most riders have no idea what low is.

Uses: Absorbing high spots, setting up for tight turns, preparing to brake hard, generating downforce for pumps, hops and jumps.

All the way forward

Goal: Get all the way forward. All the way. Crouch low and get your head over the hub. Stand tall and get your hips to the bars. Most riders have no idea what forward is.

Uses: Going up steep slopes (even small ones like this), preloading the front end for manuals and hops, jumping steep lips.

All the way back

Goal: Be able to get all the way back — all the way, with low torso and straight arms — quickly and fluidly.

Uses: Pretty much everything including braking, manualing, fast drops, pumping and jumping.

Alert! This position is extremely important to every mountain biker. Practice it. Make sure the cranks, feet and rider rotate back as a unit.

Side to side

Goal: Lean the bike freely below you, *independently* of your body. The farther you can lean your bike, the tighter you can turn.

Uses: Turning!

Rotate

Goal: Let the bike rotate below you while your body goes straight where you want to go.

Uses: Any loose/rough situation where the bike is bouncing around below you (stay balanced and let the bike do its thing). Transitioning between corners.

Cyclocross racers are the masters of fast, fluid dismounts and mounts. The best don't lose any speed when they run across obstacles.

MOUNT AND DISMOUNT

Goal: Dismount and remount your bike quickly, efficiently and safely.

Uses: Safely and quickly crossing an unrideable or potentially dangerous trail section. The winning pass at the NorCal League 2005 Championship Girl's Varsity race was made by a rider who graceful dismounted and ran across a sandy section that her competitor tried to ride across!

Start by practicing these skills at low speed on smooth ground, then gradually practice them faster and on real terrain.

Rolling dismount

1. Slow down to a safe speed. Unclip your right foot and swing it behind your bike. Always dismount to the left.

2. Swing your right foot forward betwen your left foot and the bike.

3. As you set your right foot onto the ground, unclip your left foot and hit the ground running, right foot first.

Rolling mount

1. Run alongside your bike and thrust yourself upward with your left leg. Swing your right leg over your saddle.

2. Land on your right inner thigh. Be careful not to land in the wrong place! Try not to plop down onto the saddle. Instead, try to slide onto it. Make the movement less vertical and more horizontal.

3. Find your right pedal and push down. Catch your left pedal as it crosses the top of your stroke, then rip it!

CRASH SAFELY

Mastering Mountain Bike Skills 2nd Edition has an entire chapter on preventing injuries.

The best cure for crashing is prevention. Focus on great skills, and always ride within your limits. That said, here are some things to consider about crashing:

Try to ride it out. If you feel a slight buck or tweak, balance on your feet, get loose and let your bike do what it's designed to do, which is roll through stuff.

Bail sooner than later. If your instincts tell you you're in real trouble, get out of there *before* something bad happens. Do not hang on hoping for the best.

If you get bucked forward, get off the bike! This is important. Start running in the air. Keep your head up and try to land feet first. Either run or tumble it out.

Try to fall on the low side of the bike, rather than flopping over the top. When a turn or steep section goes wrong, lean into the inside of the turn or into the hill. This will let you down easy.

Don't try to stop yourself. Falling isn't the problem. It's the sudden stop. If you put your arms out and try to stop yourself, something might break (often your collarbone).

Run it out. This is ideal. Jump off your bike and keep running until all that wayward kinetic energy has been expressed.

Roll with it. This is where smart practice and good instincts make the difference between a nonevent and a helicopter ride. See below.

This is a good time to jump off the bike and start running.

NICA photo

Practice crashing

Yes, practice crashing. It's a skill, and the better you do it, the better your life will be. Try practicing this progression in a soft, grassy area. Add difficulty and speed very gradually, only after each level is mastered.

1. Forward roll from a kneeling position.

2. Forward roll from a standing position.

3. Forward roll while walking. Work up to a slow jog, then a quick run.

4. Jump off a moving bike then run it out.

5. Jump off a moving bike then run into a forward roll.

How to forward roll: Check out this video: http://www.youtube.com/watch?v=W93w6aw26Ls

TROUBLESHOOTING

Problem: Your arms are getting tired, and your eyes are rattling in your head. Every time you hit a bump it gets worse.

Solution: You're too far forward. Shift your hips back until your palms stop pressing on the bars and your hands are weightless. That'll keep you centered.

Problem: When you hit water bars and other obstacles at speed, especially on downhills, you feel the back end kick up. You might even get bucked over the bars. Not good.

Solution: Believe it or not, you're too far back. Shift your hips forward until your fingers stop pulling on the bars and your hands are weightless. That'll keep you centered.

Problem: Your shoulders or triceps get tired when you climb.

Solutions: You're slumping and putting too much weight on your bars. Sit up straighter and put more pressure into the pedals. Also, your bike size and stem length could be wrong. Discuss with your coach and, possibly, visit a quality shop for a fit.

Problem: On steep, seated climbs, your front tire wanders around like a balloon on a windy day.

Solution: Your weight is too far back. Crouch low and pull yourself forward until the front tire starts to track.

Problem: You struggle for balance. Maybe you find yourself swinging your bars back and forth and waving your knees all over the place as you try to make a turn or get over an outcropping.

Solutions: Relax and look as far ahead as possible. If low-speed sections give you trouble, speed up! Kidding. Sort of.

DRILLS - ATTACK POSITION PART BY PART

What they'll learn

This series of drills teaches the neutral attack position body part by body part. Coaches can run these drills in series or do them one at a time to focus on problem areas.

This is a lot of detail, but — hey — every riding skill starts with a good attack position.

Why this is important

A neutral attack position forms the foundation of all mountain bike skills. When riders can automatically find this position, they will ride all terrain with greater confidence and control. Everything your riders do on the bike starts here!

Setup

Open area with good traction where riders can do a loop around the teacher.

A slight grade lets riders coast easily.

When learning this position, consider lowering the seat to encourage greater range.

These points can (and should) be practiced on real terrain.

How to run these drills

Show the riders your best attack position. Say this is where we are going; we are going to build this position from the ground up. From a seated position, show riders, part by part, how you "build" your attack position. Feet, knees, hips, torso, shoulders, elbows, hands then finally head and eyes. As you set each part, describe what you are doing and why.

After you finish, guide your riders through the same exercise, one part at a time. For each part, describe the goal, say why it's important, show it on your bike then tell your riders to do the same. Progress through the following part-by-part drills:

> ### Showing and telling
>
> Consider having an experienced rider demonstrate on-the-bike skills as you describe the rider's form and position. Encourage questions. Repeat the demonstration as many times (in as many ways) as necessary until your riders get it.

5. Shoulders low, blades down and back

4. Torso level

3. Hips back

8. Head up, eyes out

7. Hands weightless, wrists straight

6. Elbows out

2. Knees bent

1. All weight on feet, feet parallel with cranks

DRILL - ATTACK POSITION - FEET

Goal: Feet and cranks level with horizon, feet parallel with cranks. All weight on feet. Weightless hands.

Why: This drives weight straight into bottom bracket, perpendicular with cranks. No matter what is going on, if the rider drives weight into the cranks this way, all will be good. Explain how this position changes (but stays the same) on steep ups and downs.

How: For now stand upright with feet and cranks level and hands as light as possible. This is the A-1 most important aspect of riding technique. It distributes your weight perfectly on the tires, and it lets the bike work the way it's designed to. Heavy feet, light hands!

Look for:

- Toes or heels up.
- Weight pressing into or pulling on bars.
- If you see triceps, rider is too far forward.
- If you see biceps, rider is too far back.

DRILL - ATTACK POSITION - KNEES

Goal: Keep knees slightly bent, directly below hips (neither pulled in or bowed out), and on the same plane as if they share a pivot point.

Why: Keeping the knees on same plane does a few good things: A) helps ensure rider is weighting pedals evenly, and B) rider generates equal power from both legs.

How: From the saddle, set the feet level, then put the knees next to each other, then get off the saddle. Keep knees on same plane vertically and longitudinally. Demonstrate weightless hands.

Look for:

One knee bent, the other straight, knees far from each other. Show riders this is a common mistake. "How many of you have felt this happen, especially on a gnarly downhill? … Did one leg get tired? … That's because all your weight was on one leg. … Did you feel in control? … Of course not; you weren't balanced on both feet."

One knee way in front of the other. Very common. This can be a function of tightness. Encourage riders to work on knee alignment. Bringing the hips into position helps.

See next drill.

DRILL - ATTACK POSITION - HIPS

Goal: Keep knees where they are, above and between the feet. Push hips back and let torso articulate flat.

Why: Pushing hips back recruits the powerful gluteal muscles. This hips-back position brings the shoulders down, which it the only way to gain range of motion for cornering, drops and other moves.

How: Start off the bike. Coach demonstrates. Assume athletic position, with knees bent and behind toes. Coach pushes hips back and folds torso flat. Coach shows that the knees do not come forward. All movement is in the hips. Strive for 90-degree angle between lower and upper legs, and a level torso. Demonstrate proper balance by standing on toes (or cleats) then driving hips back/torso level while staying on toes of cleats. Get riders to do the same. Most will not be able to access this position right away. Work on it.

Once riders get the idea, coach demonstrates on the bike. From the saddle, coach places feet and knees, then pushes hips back behind the seat. This brings the shoulders down and folds torso flat. Stress that you are not bringing the shoulders forward — that would shift weight onto bars — you are pushing hips back and letting shoulders come down. This shift from the saddle is critical for XC riders. Show it and explain it until riders seem to get the idea.

Have riders make the same hip shift. Set feet, set knees, push hips back and let torso fold flat.

Look for:

Hips not going back far enough. Very common, especially among growing, inflexible teens. Encourage riders to go as far as they can, but not to strain. As riders warm up they will get more mobile. If the team practices this on a regular basis, riders will get more mobile over the course of the season.

Shoulders coming forward and putting weight on bars. If you see triceps, something is wrong. Stress importance of riders getting back. Show again how your butt is behind the saddle when your torso is flat.

Riders going back too far. If you see biceps, something is wrong. This is a good problem; have riders pull themselves forward a little at a time until the hands are neutral.

Regular off-bike mobility work helps riders access full range of motion.

NICA photo

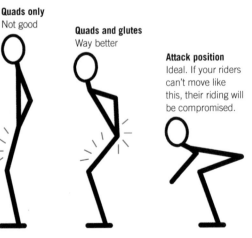

Standing

Quads only
Not good

Quads and glutes
Way better

Attack position
Ideal. If your riders can't move like this, their riding will be compromised.

DRILL - ATTACK POSITION - TORSO

Goal: Torso is as level as possible. Torso is straight and engaged.

Why: Bringing the torso level brings the shoulders down, which increases arm range of motion. A level torso (with light hands) is a sign of proper hip placement. Keeping torso neutral and engaged — and not arching or bending — improves breathing and improves stability. Remember that all forces between the bars and pedals pass through the torso. Level, straight and engaged!

How: It all comes from the hips. Do not bend at the waist. Push hips back and pivot at the hip joint. In order to stay balanced on the pedals, the rider must simultaneously bring shoulders forward and fold the torso to level.

Coach demonstrates hip shift again, calling attention to torso.

Riders practice hip shift with special attention to torso.

Look for:

- All hip issues.

- Riders bending (common) or arching (not common) at the waist. Inflexible riders will often keep their hips vertical and bend at the waist to bring shoulders down. Do not let this happen. It's better for a rider to be somewhat upright but with good hip/torso alignment than to force the shoulders low and bend at the waist. The range of motion will improve over time (with frequent practice).

A level torso brings your shoulders down and gives you the range of motion to work transitions on pump tracks and trails.

DRILL - ATTACK POSITION - SHOULDERS

Goal: Shoulders low; try for same level as hips. Shoulder blades pulled down toward hips, packed against back.

Why: Low shoulders increase arm range of motion, which is essential for cornering, braking and most other skills. Packed shoulders provide stability and strength, as well as safety for the shoulder joint.

How: Coach demonstrates [poor] cornering technique with high shoulders. Shows that lean angle and corner line are limited by lack of range of motion. Coach then lowers shoulders and rails a tight turn.

Coach hunches shoulders and asks riders how often they feel themselves riding like this. Listen for responses like "very often, especially when I'm afraid or uncomfortable." Ask riders to do pushups with shrugged shoulders. Not very easy. Coach shows riders how to pull shoulder blades down and back — really cranking 'em down with the back muscles — then relax and raise elbows. This is strong. This is how we ride. Coach tells riders to do pushups again. Better?

Coach goes through position progression on the bike. Feet, knees, hips then calls attention to the shoulder being low and the blades being pulled back.

Riders do the same.

Shoulder blades pulled toward hips.
NO HUNCHING!

Look for:

Shoulders still too high. That's tied to hip shift. See hip section.

Torso bent at waist. Also tied to hip shift.

Shoulder blades splayed outward and forward. If coach sees the inner points of the shoulder blades, the blades are not packed on the back. Get that rider off the bike. Pull shoulders down while standing next to bike. When rider gets it, go back to bike.

Many riders — actually most — have weak back muscles and rounded upper body posture. This is often related to a common condition called upper cross syndrome in which the chest muscles overpower the back muscles. Awareness and training can bring upper body into better balance and improve posture on and off the bike.

Ask riders to consider their posture during school and to practice sitting straight while in class.

Shoulders low.
Hips back and torso level.

DRILL - ATTACK POSITION - ELBOWS

Goal: Elbows out! Look for 90-degree angles between upper and lower arm and between upper arm and side of torso.

Why: Increased range of motion. Increased ability to absorb shocks. Increased ability to pull and push. Looks cool at any speed.

How: Coach stands in front of riders. From the packed shoulder blade position, coach shows riders how to bring elbows up without hunching the shoulders. Riders copy.

Coach demonstrates on bike. Riders copy.

Look for:

- Elbows in close to the body. This is very common, especially among road riders accustomed to drop bars. "Elbows out!" often gets their attention.

- Elbows in front of shoulders. This is rare and only possible with very mobile riders (many of whom seem to be swimmers). This is weak and dangerous. Make sure elbows stay even with or slightly behind shoulders.

- Hunched shoulders. Many riders bring shoulders toward their ears when they bring their elbows out. Tell them to push shoulders as far as possible from ears, while keeping elbows out.

Elbows out! This gives you the range of motion and strength to make quick transitions, as on this pump track.

DRILL - ATTACK POSITION - HANDS

Goal: Hands neutral. Neither pulling nor pushing. Wrists straight. No bend in the wrists.

Why: If hands are light and rider is off saddle, that means all weight is in the feet, where it belongs.

Pulling or pushing through bent wrists is weak, uncomfortable and dangerous.

How:

See all cues for heavy feet.

Coach demonstrates what happens if hands grab bars in sitting position then stand without adjusting grip. Wrists are bent. Ask riders, would they lift a heavy object with bent wrists? Coach then shows how to loosen and adjust grip when rider goes from sitting to standing (and vice versa) to keep wrists straight.

Riders do the same.

Look for:

- Signs of pulling or pushing on the bars. Adjust fore-aft balance by shifting hips forward or back. Heavy feet, light hands!

- Bent wrists. Look at riders' wrists in all riding situations. Call attention to bent wrists.

- Squeezing the bars or complaining of sore hands. Advise riders to keep their hands loose and relaxed. Strive for "tea party fingers."

Demonstrate light hands,
loose grip, straight wrists.

DRILL - ATTACK POSITION - HEAD AND EYES

Goal: Head is up. Rider is leading with chin.

Eyes are out and scanning as far ahead as possible.

Why: Human vestibular systems are designed for upright posture.

Riders can only ride where they've seen, and they can only ride as fast as they can see. Proper vision is hugely important because it helps you:

- identify the best line for you.
- give your brain the information it needs to direct your body.
- recognize other trail users well in advance.

How:

Coach demonstrates proper head position and stresses importance of looking ahead. Coach identifies a reference point 50 feet ahead of the riders.

Riders assume attack position and look directly at the ground under their front wheels, then they look at the reference point. Coach asks which felt better, which felt faster or slower. Coaches should pay attention to rider vision in all situations.

Look for:

- Head facing down. Lead with the chin!
- Eyes locked on the front tire or "trouble" spots like turns or rocks. Give riders specific places to look. They should be as far ahead as possible.

Encourage riders to look all the way *through* the turns. As soon as possible, look at the *next* turn.

Working the hips-back
drill at a NorCal Leaders'
Summit. Try this with your
team.

NICA photo

4

PEDAL EFFICIENTLY

Goals:

- Help riders pedal comfortably.

- Embrace pedaling as a skill.

- Encourage riders to spin high rpm.

- Develop efficient technique both in and out of the saddle.

- Sprint intelligently.

- Teach a reliable power stroke.

- Make sure riders understand shifting.

GOALS FOR PEDALING

The pedaling wisdom in this chapter comes from a crew of distinguished experts at the Boulder Center for Sports Medicine, including: Lester Pardoe (biomechanical technician), Rob Pickels (exercise physiologist) and Sean Madsen (cycling biomechanist).

Goals for pedaling

Comfort. Bike and shoes fit you well, and you can ride without strain or injury.

Efficiency. Get max power and endurance from a given level of fitness or energy.

Power. Develop more power, and learn to use it to ride better and faster.

Adaptability. Learn to pedal well in all situations:

Embrace pedaling as a skill. Many riders think of pedaling only in terms of fitness. They are doing themselves a disservice. Work capacity is largely genetic. Fitness is transitory. Great technique makes everyone smoother, more comfortable and eventually faster. Focus on great technique while developing power and endurance. You'll end up with happier (and faster) riders.

If you have access to indoor spin bikes or stationary trainers, consider conducting clinics where you focus on pedaling techniques.

Spin it, spin it good

Encourage your riders to spin easy gears quickly, rather than mash hard gears slowly. Strive for an average cadence of 80-90 rpm (yes, that seems high, but it's important). Compared with chugging a big gear at 45 rpm, buzzing a small gear at 90 rpm yields these advantages:

It protects riders' knees. The lighter gear at twice the cadence places less force on young riders' growing (and fragile) knees. Hard gears and high forces squeeze synovial fluid out of the space between the leg bones, causing cartilage to grind directly on cartilage. For this reason NICA forbids single speeds from competition, and we strongly encourage you to keep your riders from training on single speeds.

It saves muscle power for when they need it. Easy gears and high rpms leave legs fresher for technical climbs and glorious finishes.

It's more efficient. With the pedals moving quickly, there are fewer dead spots and a smoother overall stroke. This improves traction, lengthens endurance and allows riders to lay down more power.

Suffering is optional

Learn the difference between working hard and working incorrectly.

It's OK (and expected) to hurt while you pedal your hardest. Just make sure you're also pedaling your best. This is more efficient, faster — and more fun.

When riders learn something new, they often slow down at first. Studies show, however, if they stick with the new technique they will improve over the long run.

IN THE SADDLE

This the most efficient place to generate long-term power. Encourage your riders to do most of their pedaling in the saddle. Tips to get around the stroke:

Up: Studies show that pulling up at cycling speeds is useless. Relax. Have a short rest. Focus on the opposite downstroke — and on driving across the top.

Across the top: Focus on dropping your heel, engaging the pedal ASAP and driving across the top of the stroke. This starts the power phase earlier.

Down: The power phase. Drive downward with the heel. Use your glutes.

Across the bottom: Focus on pushing the other foot across the top. Trying to pull back only helps at very low rpm.

Watch your riders' heels:

Here Lester is pedaling easily at 90 rpm. At lower rpm in a harder gear, the ankle movement is more pronounced; he has to engage the pedal as much as possible.

Up:	**Across top:**	**Down:**	**Across bottom:**
Heel raises as pedal reaches top. Don't try to pull up.	Drop heel and push across top. Drive from your hip.	Drive downward through heel. End with slighty pointed toe.	Pull back slightly to finish power stroke. Focus on opposite foot.

Upper body is as quiet as possible, except:

> Pull your torso down and forward on steep climbs. See page 84.

> Brace your upper body for efficient power transfer. Firm but relaxed.

> Pull back as you push across the top. This adds to your leg power.

Change it up. On long climbs move around and use different muscles. Shift forward and focus on your quads, then scoot back and focus on your glutes and hamstrings. These shifts keep you feeling fresher.

Low-rpm training. Once or twice a week (at the max), have your team turn harder gears and lower cadences in the saddle. This builds pedaling-specific strength and teaches riders to apply more power for a longer period. For high school kids, low cadence means 60 rpm.

Upper body is relaxed.

OUT OF THE SADDLE

Climbs this steep cannot be ridden in the saddle. Get up, get forward and HAMMER!

The first question when it comes to pedaling out of the saddle is:

Why are you standing?

Almost all riders are more efficient in the saddle. Your riders should learn to do most of their pedaling in a relaxed yet powerful seated position. However, there are some good reasons to stand:

To stretch and use different muscles. Long, seated climbs have a way of making some parts tired and other parts numb. Periodic standing lets the blood flow and shifts the work to different muscles. If it feels better, do it. But keep it brief.

To stay balanced over bumps or very steep pitches. When a bike goes up a very steep slope, even if it's very short, there's no way to stay balanced while in the saddle. Stand up and balance on your feet. You'll be smoother (and usually faster).

Some lighter riders can be more efficient out of the saddle than in. The small Marco Pantani did a lot of standing climbing; the big Lance Armstrong almost always sits. Experiment. Find out what works for you.

Try to keep hips and head level. Bobbing wastes energy, especially with suspension.

Up:
Heel raises as pedal reaches top. Knee drives toward bar.

Across top:
Drop heel a bit as you start to push forward.

Down:
Extend down and back. Knee angle is almost same as sitting.

Across bottom:
Relax. Focus on pushing other foot across top.

Tighten your core. Suck in your gutt like you're gonna get punched. Pull your belly button toward your spine. This creates a stable platform for ultimate power.

Let the bike sway naturally from side to side. But: Don't *try* to sway. Stay as square as possible, without being tense. You want to be firm, yet relaxed. Tricky.

SPRINTING

If your fork or shock has a lockout: USE IT! Plan ahead so you're locked out before that victory sprint.

The first issue with sprinting is planning:

Where do you need to sprint? Pre-ride the course. Know where the finish is. Practice it several times at race speed. Choose your gears ahead of time.

Pick a ring. You do not want to shift the front derailleur during a sprint (you have to back off the power). Choose one of the bigger rings with a bigger cog, then step down the cogs using your rear shifter.

Start in an easy gear so you can spin it up quickly. Once you are spinning fast, then start upshifting. When you want to pass a semi in your car, you downshift to get the rpms up, then you start upshifting. It's the same idea on a bike.

Practice spinning faster and faster; you can get more speed out of any gear.

Accerate out of the saddle to top speed, then sit and try to maintain speed. Practice great technique both in and out of the saddle.

POWER STROKES/RATCHETING

Practice this move 100 times on a 6-inch curb before trying it on an 18-inch ledge. The smoother and more powerful the power stroke, the easier the drop. Yosei Ikeda photo

In some situations a rider needs to uncork one extra-powerful part-crank. Examples:

Surging up a ledge or water bar. You might already be pedaling pretty hard, but you need an extra boost to bring the front end up or simply clear an extra-steep section.

Ratcheting the pedals in the rocks. If you drop the pedal all the way, it will strike the ground. Keep the pedals high and working.

Wheelying off a ledge. If you can't roll off a drop, you need to keep the front end up until the rear takes off.

These part-strokes are much like the top- and down-stroke you use in the saddle:

1. Engage the freehub. Pedal softly for a half crank before you unleash the power. You should feel the chain engaged with the hub, with no slack or "clack" sound. As you reach the top of the stroke:

2. Drop your heel and push across the top. The sooner you can do this, the more power you get.

3. Push down as hard as you can and far as you dare. Up a ledge, keep pedaling. In a rock garden, backpedal and repeat. Down a ledge, keep pedaling and prepare to land.

KNOW ABOUT SHIFTING

Gear inches

Gear inches = the distance your bike rolls with one rotation of the cranks

(front gear / rear gear) x tire diameter x 3.14 = gear inches

Small/big: (22 / 34) x 26" x 3.14 = 53"

Middle/middle: (32 / 16) x 26" x 3.14 = 163"

Big/small: (44 / 11) x 26" x 3.14 = 327"

Make learning this fun and engaging by incorporating a demonstration into one of your practices. Have riders estimate how far they think the bike will roll with one turn of the crank in each gear combination. Riders can draw lines in the dirt to indicate where they think the bike will roll to before you spin the bike. Watch everyone's reactions when they see what happens!

Gear ratio

This is the practical, everyday way to think about gear inches.

(front gear / rear gear) = gear ratio

(32 / 16) = 2

Even more practical is to talk in terms of small, middle or big ring and No. X cog. The biggest cog is No. 1; the smallest is No. 8, 9 or 10 depending on the drivetrain. Come up with a team shifting language:

Hit that climb in small/1.

Pump the rocks in middle/3.

Hammer the finish straight in big/5.

Shifting 101

Shifting can be intimidating for newbies. Let's break it down:

Riders set their gear ratios by selecting the proper chain ring and cog (see diagram at right).

The ideal gear ratio lets the rider turn the pedals smoothly, efficiently and powerfully. The more low-end torque and high-end spin a rider has, the more flexible the gear choices.

Use your front shifter to fine-tune your gear ratio and keep yourself in the middle of your powerband.

Save your front shifter for major terrain changes.

> Big ring: Downhill and fast, flat riding
>
> Middle ring: Short or mellow climbs and slow, flat riding
>
> Small ring: Long or steep climbs

Keep the chain as straight as possible. Don't let it reach from one side to the other (see diagram at right).

Keep the chain as tight as possible. On downhills, a larger ring and cog make the chain tighter and less likely to bounce off the ring.

Shift before you need to. High-end rear derailleurs can handle a lot of pressure, but even the best front shifters can crumble under your awesome power. Plan ahead. Surge for half a crank, back off a bit, make your shift then get back on the throttle.

> Tip: Identify shifting points during pre-race course inspections.

When in doubt, leave it in the middle ring. Most riders in most situations don't need their small and big rings. For many beginners, it's easiest to leave the front in the middle and work the back.

> Up hills: Learn to pull the 34x34. Practice running with your bike. That's faster than the 22x34 anyway.
>
> Down hills: Use the middle ring and one of the bigger cogs. Focus on recovering from the previous climb — and pumping terrain for free speed!

If your rider can handle most rides in the middle ring, consider installing a chain guide. This will almost eliminate the possibility of a dropped chain.

Watch for riders using improper gear combinations. Discuss with them as appropriate.

These gear combos ...

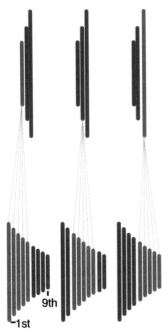

... give you all ratios

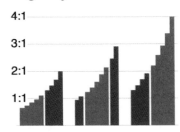

Front: 22, 32, 44t
Rear: 11, 13, 15, 17, 20, 23, 26, 30, 34t

2x10: More and more bikes are coming with 2x10 drivetrains, which means they have two rings in front and 10 cogs in back. This makes shifting simpler: Small ring when you're going slow, big ring when you're going fast.

Don't forget the cleats

Problem: Your feet pull out of the pedals unexpectedly — and frequently at really bad times.

Solution: Inspect the pedal cleats to determine if they need replacement. Be sure the pedals are adjusted properly.

TROUBLESHOOTING

Problem: No matter what you try, you can't hang with your buddies up the hills.

Solution: Train smart and ride with clean technique. If your buddies still beat you up the climbs, sorry. They might be genetically better climbers than you. But that's OK. You can learn to wax them on the descents.

Problem: The beginning of every ride hurts. A lot.

Solution: Whoa, Tiger! You can't just pin it from the parking lot. Start slowly and gradually increase the intensity. As you warm up, mix in a few short, intense bursts to wake everything up. Make sure you're sweating and ready to rock before you hit the first steep climb.

Problem: Your quads are getting really tired, but your glutes are just hanging there.

Solution: Move back on the saddle and concentrate on pushing forward from your hips. This emphasizes your glutes—the strongest muscles in your body—and provides a bit of rest to your four best friends.

Problem: You're struggling and feel really uncomfortable on a climb.

Solution: Pay attention to your form. Open your upper body, lighten your hands, and spin smooth circles. This can make a huge difference. That said, if you're going super hard or you're out of shape, it's gonna hurt. Welcome to cycling.

Problem: When you climb out of the saddle, your triceps get tired from leaning on the bars.

Solution: Move your hips back so your weight moves exclusively to your feet. For extended climbing, rest your hands neutrally on the bars. For max power, pull on the bars with each downstroke.

Problem: Your chain falls off on downhills.

Solution: Descend in your big chainring and one of the middle to larger cogs. Remove links until your chain is barely long enough for your big ring/big cog combo. If the tighter chain doesn't do the trick, think about installing a chain guide.

Problem: Your riders feel tired and weak.

Solution: Provide training plans, and encourage riders to follow them.

DRILL - BASIC SEATED PEDALING

What they'll learn

Riders will learn to improve their seated pedaling strokes.

Why it's important

The more efficiently your riders can pedal, the more comfortable they'll be, the longer they can ride and they faster they can rip.

Setup

Long, slight uphill with paved or hardpacked surface.

This can also be done on an indoor trainer.

How to run this drill

Have riders select a gear that lets them turn 60 rpm* with moderate resistance. This is not about intensity; it's about perfection.

Do repeats of the hill, focusing on these points in this order:

Ankling. Riders' ankles should move as the pedals turn. Heel down across the top and driving down, toe down across the bottom and coming up. Look for about 20 degrees of ankle rotation.

Pushing across the top. As early as possible on the upstroke, focus on dropping the heel then pushing forward across the top.

Quiet upper body. While riders do the above, the upper body is relaxed but braced.

Single-legged pedaling. (Turbo) This forces riders to be active all the way around the circle. Riders do 10 strokes with one leg, 10 strokes with both legs, 10 strokes with the other leg, etc. Riders must be clipped in. Riders will need easier gears.

Things to look for

Stiff ankles. Whether feet are level, pointed up or pointed down (common), encourage riders to cycle them as they pedal. See the pedaling chapter of this manual.

Late downstroke. Listen to the tires. If you hear the growl at 3 o'clock, that's too late. Some single-legged pedaling will fix that.

Noisy upper body. Tell riders to hold their upper bodies up with core muscles and let their hands hover weightlessly on the bars.

Bouncing in saddle. Focus on low cadence, then gradually build up the speed.

Faster and faster

As riders get smooth at low rpms, do intervals at higher and higher cadences. This will gradually help riders feel comfortable spinning quickly and smoothly.

Lester Pardoe drives downward with his heel. Note the relaxed upper body.

*Have riders count the number of times their right knee comes up in 15 seconds of pedaling. Multiply this number by four and that is the total rpm. Clearly instruct riders when to start and stop counting.

DRILL - BASIC STANDING PEDALING

Straight arms!

Most riders bend at their waists and pull with bent arms. Encourage them to stand tall and brace with straight arms. It's way better!

Lester Pardoe extends above his pedals.

What they'll learn

Riders will learn to improve their standing pedaling strokes.

Why it's important

The more efficiently your riders can pedal, the more comfortable they'll be, the longer they can ride and they faster they can rip. Pedaling out of the saddle offers rest on long climbs and power for steep/technical sections.

Setup

Long, slight uphill with paved or hardpacked surface.

How to run this drill

Have riders select a gear that lets them turn 60 rpm out of the saddle with moderate resistance. This is not about intensity; it's about perfection.

Do repeats of the hill, focusing on these points in this order:

Balance. Riders should be extended above their pedals, with no weight on the bars. It's OK to pull on the bars for extra power, but it's never OK to rest on the bars.

Ankling. Riders' ankles should move as the pedals turn. Heel down across the top and driving down, toe down across the bottom and coming up. Look for about 20 degrees of ankle rotation.

Pushing across the top. As early as possible on the upstroke, focus on dropping the heel then pushing forward across the top.

Level upper body. Torso and head should not bounce up and down. Tip: The more engaged the upstroke, the less the body comes up with the pedal.

Higher rpm. As riders get smooth at low cadences, have them spin for short periods as fast as they can *smoothly*. This extends the powerband and leads to race-winning sprints.

Things to look for

Weight on the hands. Look for bulging triceps. Moderate climbs should be doable without hands. Steeper climbs benefit from pulling back (not up) on bars in opposition to pushing pedal across the top.

Stiff ankles. Have riders exaggerate the ankle motion. 20 degrees is ideal.

Clunking freehubs. A sign of a disengaged topstroke and late downstroke.

Bouncing. Have rider pick a reference point and don't let eyes move up and down.

DRILL - BASIC SPRINTING

What they'll learn

Riders will learn to plan and execute race-winning sprints.

Why it's important

An inch can win a race. A surge of power can keep a mountain biker riding instead of walking.

Setup

Long, slight uphill with paved or hardpacked surface.

If you know your race finishes are flat, do sprint practice on flat ground.

How to run this drill

Mark out a sprint zone. Start with 100 yards and work up to 200 yards.

Riders will roll into the sprinting zone at race speed (basically their highest sustainable pace) then accelerate to max speed.

Find a gear that riders can spin easily and accelerate from race speed on the given grade. As a rule, riders should start the sprint at about 80 rpm then wind it up from there (the faster your riders can spin, the faster they can sprint).

Have riders enter the sprint zone at race speed then stand and hammer as hard as they can. They should accelerate to the highest smooth cadence they can turn, then upshift. Riders should stand as long as they are accelerating. When they hit their max speed, they should sit and try to maintain as long as they can.

Let riders fully recover before repeating this drill. Expect it to be hard.

Things to look for

Shifting too early. Most riders, especially kids, upshift then try to pull hard gears, thinking this is fast. It's actually quite slow. Focus on accelerating as much as possible with spin, then upshifting.

Bouncing and sloppy pedaling. Smooth is fast. Revisit standing pedaling technique. Encourage riders to quiet their bodies and only put effort where it counts.

Riders blowing up before the end of the sprint. We want riders to push through pain, but we don't want them to have negative experiences. Shorten the sprint zone to ensure quality.

Still accelerating at the end of the zone. That's a great problem to have. Make the sprint zone longer.

Encourage your riders to refine their pedaling and sprinting techniques. A powerful sprint might get them on a podium some day!

NICA photo

5

CONTROL SPEED

Goals:

- Make sure riders understand why and when to brake.

- Teach perfect braking technique. Important!

- Help riders identify effective braking points on trails and race courses.

- Learn to minimize trail wear through effective and responsible braking.

PREPARE TO BRAKE

Entering an unknown drop is a great time to use your brakes. With practice, you can ride sections like this with no weight at all on your hands (note the Tea Party fingers). This gives you perfect balance to brake harder, let it roll, deal with bumps, make a turn or whatever.

vastaction.com photo

Most mountain bike injuries that require hospitalization stem from uncontrolled speed. Teaching riders how to control their speed is a major way to keep them safe and to prevent avoidable crashes.

Effective braking also makes riders faster. The less time they spend braking, the faster they go. Be sure to instruct riders to maintain safe and socially responsible riding speeds.

Good reasons to brake:

To control your speed. If you feel like you're going too fast, by all means slow down.

To scrub speed for a technical section or corner. You DO NOT want to hit the brakes in that rock garden or loose corner. Slow down before the section. Slow down so much you feel bored (so there's no chance you'll panic and grab the levers), then build speed through the section.

For balance demonstration
Don't actually ride with no hands!

To ride within your vision. You should only ride as fast as you can see. If you can't see around a turn, slow down so you can react to whatever (or whomever) you encounter.

> **Exception:** On a prepped race course, go as fast as you can. Be ready for anything.

Bad reasons to brake:

You have nothing better to do and you feel like you should be doing something. There's always something to do. If you're not pedaling, cornering or pumping, you should be braking hard — then getting back to pedaling, cornering or pumping.

You are nervous. If you have a specific reason to slow down, please slow down. If not, focus on good body position and working the terrain. When it's time to brake, brake hard and get it done, then get back to riding.

BRAKE WITH POWER AND CONTROL

The key to proper braking is … surprise …body position. Shift your weight back so your weight drives into your pedals, not your hands.

1. Low attack position. The lower you get, the farther back you can get, and the harder you can brake. And: The lower you get, the better you can handle bumps, drops, turns, etc.

2. Gradually squeeze both levers. Always both. As the braking force builds up, rotate your entire body back around your bottom bracket.

3. Squeeze the levers hard and drive all force into your feet.

4. Gradually release the levers and return to your attack position. Light hands!

Don't skid: Practice modulating braking pressure to get the most braking power without skidding.

Load the tires: To dramatically increase your traction and braking power, push the tires into the ground as you squeeze the levers.

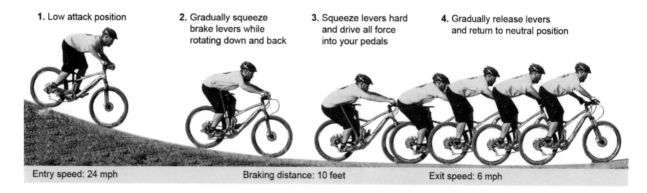

1. Low attack position

2. Gradually squeeze brake levers while rotating down and back

3. Squeeze levers hard and drive all force into your pedals

4. Gradually release levers and return to neutral position

Entry speed: 24 mph   Braking distance: 10 feet   Exit speed: 6 mph

This position is critical!

Get back. Way back. Farther. This is flat, smooth ground. On a steep slope the rider has to be even farther back. Short stems make this easier.

Rotate feet and cranks back. This drives the net force into the feet. If you can't do this, your weight will shear forward onto your handlebars.

Weight perpendicular to crankset. This is the key to good balance and good times.

Yosei Ikeda photos

When you need to control your speed in a really steep/rocky section, look for spots where you can brake safely.

Brake hard. Drive the net force into your pedals. Let go of the brakes. Get back to working the terrain.

Farid Tabaian photo

DECIDE WHERE TO BRAKE

Once you learn to brake well, you learn you only need a small patch of good ground to slow down. In the sequence on the previous page, the bike slows from 24 to 6 mph in only 10 feet.

On or off. Many riders treat their brakes like a dimmer switch; they drag them 50% all the way down the hills. Brakes are like light switches: They should either be on or off. Choose where to brake. Brake hard. Get back to riding.

Slow way down. Rather than trying to maintain, say, 10 mph down a long hill, let it go faster in the easy spots and slow down even more in the scary spots. There's a time to go fast, and there's a time to go slow. When it's time to go slow, brake hard. Get it done. Get back to riding.

Brake before corners. Not in them.

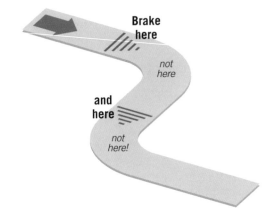

Brake before rocks and ledges. Not on them.

Practice braking once per section. Slow down enough that you're focused on being smooth and building speed, not worrying about controlling speed.

On your trails and race tracks, identify braking points ahead of time. Practice braking only in those spots.

Practice maximal braking on pavement, then different kinds of dirt. As riders improve, add steep slopes and bumps. A skilled rider can stop riding down a stairway with weightless hands. Heavy feet, light hands!

TROUBLESHOOTING

Problem: Your rear tire skids.

Solution: You are probably too far forward. Squeeze the levers slowly. Make sure you shift your weight back so your weight is in your feet and your hands are light. Heavy feet, light hands!

Problem: Your front tire skids. (With your front tire, any skidding is bad skidding.)

Solution: If you're squeezing both brakes evenly and your front wheel is skidding, your weight might be too far back. You can tell by the pulling sensation on your fingers. Shift your weight forward until your hands are neutral — neither pushing on the palms nor pulling with the fingers. If the trail is too loose for hard braking, ease off both brakes.

Problem: On rough terrain your front wheel gets stuck and pitches you forward.

Solution: Use the brakes in the smooth sections, and absolutely, positively stay off them while your front wheel rolls over the rough parts.

Problem: When you do lots of serious downhilling, your knuckles ache. The backs of your forearms might burn as well.

Solution: Adjust your brake levers closer to your grips so you don't have to reach as far.

Problem: On long descents, your forearms are pumping and your eyes are rattling out of your head.

Solution: Shift your body down and back, so all the force drives into your pedals — not your grips. Relax!

Problem: You can't stop yourself from braking in a downhill turn. That usually doesn't turn out very well.

Solution: This is very common. Before you reach the turn, slow way down. Slow down so much you have no fear of speed. Take a late apex line. Lean the bike as much as you can to get the turning done quickly, then coast out of the turn.

(continued on next page)

Problem: You can't stop yourself from braking in a rocky/rooty section. That almost always ends poorly.

Solutions: 1) Slow way down before the section. Slow down so much you're not afraid of speed, then consciously DO NOT brake. 2) Rather than hold on for dear life and hope for the best, take control of the situation. Actively pump the bumps. This works fo well you'll start to look for rough sections. 3) If you cannot wrap your head around riding the section well, go around it or carry your bike through it. Walking is faster (and more fun) than crashing.

Problem: You take a while to slow down. You might find yourself dragging the brakes at half power. (Coaches: Watch your riders' braking behavior).

Solution: This is very common. Before you reach the turn, slow way down. Slow down so much you have no fear of speed. Take a late apex line. Lean the bike as much as you can to get the turning done quickly, then coast out of the turn.

Problem: You grab the brakes all the time, for no real reason. The levers are like your little security blankets.

Solution: This is a bad, potentially dangerous habit. 1) Learn to brake very hard and stop your bike in the smallest distance possible. This will give you confidence that you can control your speed. 2) Focus on something beneficial. Pumping is a great way to keep your mind and body engaged with the trail.

Problem: Your brakes don't seem to work as well as you remember.

Solution: The pads may be worn and in need of replacement. Be sure to inspect brake pads every month and after particularly wet or muddy rides.

Braking Bump Bonus! Tip: It's often best to skim over the bumps, brake hard then rail the turn. On a crowded race course, this can lead to a free pass.

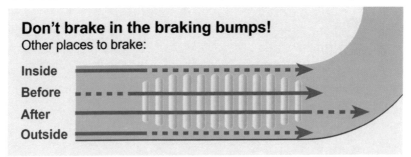

Don't brake in the braking bumps!
Other places to brake:

Inside
Before
After
Outside

DRILL - BRAKING - GET BACK

What they'll learn

How to rotate their bodies back on the bike so they can drive braking forces into the pedals rather than the handlebar.

Why it's important

This position is essential to effective braking.

Setup

Smooth, slightly sloped area where riders can ride a loop. Lower seat to help riders access the position, then raise seat to riding height.

How to run the drill

1. Explain the physics of braking and why the rider must get back and direct the net force into the pedals and cranks.

2. Demonstrate hard braking several times. Tell the riders to focus on these points, in order: A) You start in low attack position. The lower you are, the farther back you can get. B) Your feet and cranks rotating back. C) Your hips way back over the rear wheel. D) Your torso low and arms straight.

3. Tell riders to get a bit of speed and, while coasting straight, practice getting back. DO NOT BRAKE at this point. Focus on rotating the body, feet and cranks back as far as possible, with weight driving equally through both feet.

4. Have riders practice moving smoothly between low attack position and all the way back. The quicker and more fluid they are, the better they can brake — as well as go down ledges and pump terrain.

Things to look for

Level cranks and/or feet. Most riders don't rotate their cranks back, and most keep their feet too level with the horizon.

Rider too high. When rider is high on the bike and extends arms, the rider pushes the body upward, not backward. Make sure riders start this movement as low as possible, and that they push themselves back, not up.

Arms bent. If the arms are bent, the rider is not as far back as possible. Stress that riders practice this with straight arms. They should feel like they're hanging off the back of the bike.

Straight arms!

Most riders bend at their waists and pull with bent arms. Encourage them to stand tall and brace with straight arms. It's way better!

If your riders aren't this far back, they aren't far back enough.

This might look crazy, but it's perfect braking form. All force is driving through the feet into the middle of the bike. Bike geometry is stable (and fork is flexing!) Yosei Ikeda photo

DRILL - BASIC BRAKING

What they'll learn

How to control speed with perfect balance and control.

Why it's important

Proper braking lets riders handle most terrain confidently and safely.

Setup

Paved area with slight downslope to help riders gain speed. Set up a loop with a designated area to gain speed, an area for braking and a path to return to the acceleration area. Make sure all riders can access the "get back" position. Make sure riders' brake levers are set up correctly.

How to run the drill

Re-explain the physics of braking and stress the importance of rocking back with the cranks. Explain that riders must brake with the index fingers only, and that they must squeeze and release the levers gradually — while they adjust position.

Demonstrate hard braking several times. Tell riders to focus on these points, in order.
A) You start in low attack position. The lower you are, the farther back you can get.
B) Squeezing the levers. Show the timing and the squeezing tension. When you want to slow down, squeeze hard. C) Your feet and cranks rotating back. C) Your hips way back over the rear wheel. D) Your torso low and arms straight. E) The power and quickness of your braking, and the fact you didn't skid.

Have riders ride the route you set up and demonstrate their best braking technique in front of you. As they turn laps, have them focus on the points you just showed them until they are braking smoothly.

As riders master the basic form, encourage them to brake harder. By learning how little space they need to slow down, they will gain confidence on trails.

Things to look for

Issues with the backward position. See "Get Back" drill on previous page.

Rear wheel skidding. Sure sign that some force is going into the bars. Check position. Even if the body is back perfectly, one level foot will send force forward.

Lever squeeze and body shift not in sync. Many riders will move back then pull the levers or vice versa. Encourage riders to execute these moves together. It's all about timing and balance.

Starting off with perfect form then, when the brakes start working, surrendering into bad form. Super common. Encourage riders to get used to the forces — and trust their bikes and themselves.

Options

After riders dial in their paved braking, try hard packed dirt, then loose dirt and gravel. Eventually, work your way up to steep. bumpy slopes.

Measure: Coast down a steep slope for consistent speed, then start braking at a fixed point. Work on stopping in the shortest possible distance.

6

CORNER CONFIDENTLY

Goals:

- Teach the essential skills for every turn.
- Learn how to make major turns.
- Link mellower turns

Camber thrust
A leaned tire rolls like an ice cream cone

Inner diameter: ~24.3"
Outer diameter: ~25.5"

When you lean your bike, you *must* let the bars turn on their own.

ESSENTIAL IN EVERY TURN

Cornering is the most complex area of mountain biking. The core skills in this chapter will help your riders handle all corners more confidently.

For the love of all that is holy, PLEASE drive these points into your riders:

1. Low attack position! Low attack position! Low attack position! The only way to turn a bike is to lean it. The only way to lean your bike is to get low. Lower!

2. Lean your bike! That's the only way to turn. Steering is for tricycles.

3. Let your bars do what they want. When you lean your bike, the steering column turns on its own. You must let this hapen. Light hands!

4. Look past the turn. Plan your next turn. Trust the bike to do what it's made to do.

Whether you're edging into a precarious switchback or railing a perfect sweeper, the essential skills remain the same.

Practice the core skills in this chapter until they become automatic. This way, when riders encounter a scary turn (or a perfect one), they'll be ready.

vastaction.com photos

One arm very bent, one arm very straight

MAKING A MAJOR TURN

For major turns, say more than 60 degrees, you need to create angles and set edges. Here are the key steps:

1. Attack position

2. Look through the turn

3. Lean the bike

4. Turn the hips *Smile*

1. Low attack position

This turn has a gradual, fading entrance. That's why the rider is already leaning a bit and driving his upper body into the turn.

The tighter the turn, the more you have to lean and the lower you have to get. Lowness also lets you deal with bumps.

When in doubt: Get low. Lower!

Lower is better

Your brain should be working on the *next* turn

2. Look through the turn

As you reach the spot where you'll initiate the turn, try to look all the way through the exit of the turn, all the way to the entrance of the *next* turn. This skill is best practiced in a parking lot or large grass field.

This turn goes around a hill. The rider is trying to look *through* the hill.

The farther ahead you can look, the better. This reduces perceived speed and takes your mind off details like speed, distance and surface. These details challenge the conscious mind, but your body will naturally adapt if you are loose and ready.

The sooner you can identify the next turn, the sooner you hand this turn over to your peripheral vision and motor systems.

Lean bike more
than body.

3. Lean your bike

The only way to turn a bike is to lean it. The tighter the turn, the more you have to lean. If your riders can't lean their bikes, they can't turn well.

Push your inside grip down into the turn. That's how you start the movement. Enter in a low attack position with very bent arms. When it's time to turn, straighten your inside arm.

Drive all your weight into your outside pedal. This style of turn is very much like classic alpine ski turning teachnique. It's all about creating edges and driving your weight into the outside (downhill) ski.

Get the timing: As you push your inside bar into the turn, sink onto your outside foot and drive all your weight into the pedal. Make these movements smooth yet powerful.

Heavy foot, light hands!

Do not lean your body into the turn. Lean the bike below you.

Let the bars turn however they want. They know better than you do.

Practice this transition

There's a time to go straight, and there's a time to turn. When it's time to turn, TURN! Lean your bike, set your angles and get it done. Never apologize your way into a corner. Own it!

Try not to brake in turns

Before the turn, slow down so much you feel no urge to grab the brakes.

If you have to slow down in a corner, straighten your bike for a moment, brake hard then resume turning.

Inside arm
very bent

Inside arm
very straight

Looking even farther through the turn.
By now the eyes have seen the next turn, the brain knows where to go, and the body is doing all the calculations to get there.

4. Turn your hips

We're calling this step No. 4, but eventually your riders will integrate their kung fu so much they will lean their bikes, set their outside feet and turn their hips simultaneously. This will happen gracefully and powerfully at the moment of turn initiation.

Do not twist your shoulders into the turn. The shoulders and head follow the hips.

Drive from the hips. Torso stays firm. The big hip muscles drive in the new direction. Torso and head follow.

There's a flashlight in your belly button. Point it where you want to go.

Many riders lack the mobility and body awareness to execute this movement. Practice it off the bike, first on two feet, then on one.

Practice this transition

When it's time to turn, TURN! Remember?

As you enter the turn, as soon as possible, orient your upper body toward the next turn. Drive from the hips. Heavy foot, light hands!

Hips in line with bike

Hips, torso and head aimed at *next* turn!

A fun application of the hip turn (and other techniques).

Head goes as straight as possible

Low

Push bike into turn

Pull yourself low

Push bike into turn

Pull yourself low

Push bike into turn

LINKING MELLOWER TURNS

Most turns on real trails don't change direction very much. These turns emphasize staying neutral, moving the bike beneath you and making smooth transitions.

Low attack position. The tighter and quicker the turns, the lower you must be.

Keep your feet and cranks level. You can switch feet as you switch sides (it helps you set harder edges), but those movements are tricky in quick transitions.

Keep your head straight. Send your head and torso as straight and level as possible. Do not bounce up and down between turns.

Stay low and lean the bike below you. Control your bike angle with your arms.

Let the bike follow its natural arcs. If you want to turn tighter, lean more!

Expert style: Push the bike into the beginning of each turn, then pull it back to neutral and push it into the next turn. This adds traction and, eventually, pump.

Advanced drill: http://www.leelikesbikes.com/how-to-pump-a-flat-surface.html

Head floating down the trail

Your tires use the banking for traction.

Your head and upper body go as straight forward as possible.

Head goes straight

Bike swings below

This uphill slalom pump drill teaches smoothness. As your riders become more fuid with basic slalom, tell them to actively push into and pull out of each turn.

Most real turns use some combination of the "major" and "mellow" techniques.
Teach and drill both, then encourage riders to mix and match to suit trail conditions.

TROUBLESHOOTING

Problem: When you start a turn, you go kind of straight—until the end where you try extra hard and crash.

Solution: This is very common. First make sure that you enter the turn in your low attack position. Lean the bike and let the bars turn (going straight comes from not letting the bars steer naturally; that final crash comes from steering them too much).

Problem: You feel yourself falling to the inside of a turn. Heck, you might actually hit the deck.

Solution: You're leaning too much for your speed and the tightness of the turn. Lean less or go faster. Encourage your riders, as they demonstrate good technique, to go faster.

Problem: You blast straight through the turn. You might feel yourself tensing up and hitting the brakes as you follow a tangent into a tree.

Solutions: Most of the time, merely leaning the bike more will do the trick. Just pitch your bike into the corner, and it'll probably come around. If that doesn't work for ya, try slowing down and following a gentler arc. Also, always, always, always look where you want to go, out past the exit of the turn.

Problem: Your front wheel washes out.

Solutions: Chances are you're nervous and leaning back on your bike (the natural instinct: push your brain away from danger!). Enter the turn with weightless hands. If your front tire starts to go, gently shift your weight forward onto the bars until your front tire resumes tracking. As long as your front tire is doing its job, your rear tire can do what it wants.

Problem: You have trouble making flat and off-camber turns.

Solutions: Lean your bike more and weight the outside pedal. Pick smoother lines. Load your tires for temporary extra traction.

Problem: In berms, you find yourself steering up the banks to stay on course.

Solution: You're going too slow! Either speed up or ride lower in the berm, where it isn't so steep.

Problem: You freak out whenever your tires break loose.

Solution: Either slow down so you don't drift, or practice drifting in a controlled situation. This is a natural part of mountain biking; we suggest you get used to it!

Problem: When you try to lean your bike to the left, your seat hits your left inner thigh and the bike won't lean.

Solution: This is very common with high seats. As you begin your turn, stand on the outside (in this case right) foot and rotate your hips toward the end of the turn. If you turn your hips into the turn, your left leg will also point into the turn. This gives your saddle room to move. Lean the bike below you and set your left thigh on the seat.

Problem: When you try to ride linked turns, your whole body goes up and down in and out of the turns. You can feel this slowing you down, plus it feels sketchy.

Solution: You are too high and stiff. Get low. Lean the bike below you by straightening your inside arm. Work on smoothly transitioning from turn to turn. Your arms should be working and the bike should be moving side to side, but your head and torso should stay as still as possible.

DRILL - MAJOR TURN

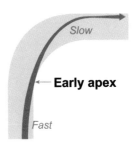

What they'll learn

Key components of executing a major turn (direction change > about 60 degrees).

Why it's important

Mountain bike trails turn. This helps riders turn reliably and safely.

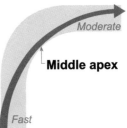

Setup

Place two cones about 15 paces apart on a smooth, flat area (pavement, packed dirt, low grass). Cones farther apart creates room for big groups and gives more time between turns. Cones closer together teach quick, precise transitions.

How to run the drill

Riders will make 180-degree turns around the cones. Start counterclockwise. When riders are smooth, switch to clockwise. Work up to figure eights (the ultimate).

This drill is broken into five sub-lessons. They go in this order:

Lean the bike - Enter in low attack position. Extend inside arm to lean bike below body.

Drop outside foot - As bike is leaned, weight shifts onto the outside foot and outside pedal goes to 6 o'clock.

Turn hips - As bike is leaned and outside pedal is dropped, the hips and torso drive in the new direction.

Get your riders to exaggerate their form. It's the best way to learn, and it can be useful in tight corners on real trails.

Find reference points - As rider reaches turning point, eyes scan ahead to next turning point. The two turning points are the only places riders should think about looking.

Choose smart lines - Riders should practice late apex lines, which are smartest and safest in most situations.

Coach demonstrates each sub-lesson while explaining what and why. Riders then ride the loop focusing on that specific skill. Coach encourages riders to build each skill on the previous ones until riders are turning beautiful laps showing all skills.

Pumping uphill

Low

Push
bike
into
turn

Pull
yourself
low

Push
bike
into
turn

Pull
·yourself
low

Push
bike
into
turn

DRILL - SLALOM TURNS

What they'll learn

How to make quick turns and smoothly transition between them.

Why it's important

Most mountain bike turns aren't major. They're more sinuous and flowy.

Setup

On a smooth, flat area, place eight or more cones five paces apart and offset one pace to the side. This makes a fun, easy slalom course.

How to run the drill

Coach explains that major turns (>60 degrees) are about creating angles and setting edges, but most turns don't change direction very much. Can the riders name trails with flowy/slalomy turns? These turns are about staying centered and moving the bike fluidly below the rider.

Coach explains/demonstrates, then riders do the same:

Step 1: Send head straight and let the bike turn below the body. Rider enters in low attack postition and actively straighten the inside arm to make each turn. As rider goes through section, the arms alternate from being very bent to very straight. Strive for smothness and fluidity.

Step 2: Rider actively pushes bike into turn and pulls bike out of turn. This increases downforce/traction, speeds transitions and leads to pump. The pull and push should be cyclical; the entire slalom is one continuous movement.

Step 3: Rider maintains or gains speed by pumping the turns. This builds on the previous steps, but is more powerful.

NOTE: If your riders can smoothly ride figure eights and pump slalom turns, they have the core cornering skills to ride well anywhere.

Look for

Riders' heads bobbing up and down. Encourage them to keep their heads level and push and pull the bike into and out of the turns.

Riders' torsos staying parallel with their bikes. Encourage riders to send their torsos straight, while the bike rotate beneath them.

Riders losing all their speed. This is a sign of fighting the bike. Many riders can't simply relax; they do better when they actively push and pull.

7

HANDLE ANY TERRAIN

Goals:

- Drive home the three keys to smoothness.
- Help riders master body position as it relates to common terrain challenges:
  - Ride down and up steep slopes.
  - Ride down and up ledges.
- Teach the world of pump.
  - Dial in pumping skills on smooth rollers.
  - Apply pump to real terrain.

THE KEYS TO SMOOTHNESS IN THE ROUGHNESS

Try to send your head and torso as straight and level as possible. There's a whole lot of complexity here, but the basic keys are:

1. Stay balanced over your feet. To the outside observer you'll be forward, back and all over the place. To you, you're standing on your feet and moving the bike.

2. Match bike angle to terrain angle. If the terrain points down, point your bike down. It the terrain points up, point your bike up. Keep your torso level with the horizon.

3. Actively work the terrain. Crouch low on the tall spots. Stand tall in the low spots.

This chapter shows some common situations you and your riders will encounter. Master the basics first. The advanced stuff will come on its own.

RIDE DOWN A STEEP SLOPE

As always, stay on top of your pedals. As the slope steepens, gradually shift your body back just enough to keep your feet heavy and your hands neutral.

- If you're pushing on the bars, you're too far forward.

- If you're pulling on the bars, you're too far back.

Get low. Lower. On a steep slope you need maximum arm range to push your bike into the drop. As you approach the edge of the drop, get as low as you can.

If the transition is abrupt, PUSH your bars into the downslope. Don't wait for the front wheel to pull you down — push it down!

If the slope can't be rolled safely, find another way down. Later you'll learn to manual or wheelie off.

If the slope is bumpy and/or you're on the brakes, you have to get even farther back (and even lower) to drive the net force into your feet.

Left: When you ride a very steep descent on a long-cockpit trail bike, it can be hard to get far enough back. Get as low as you can and extend your arms all the way into the drop.

Bottom: Whatever happens, try to stay balanced on both pedals. Short stems make it easier.

Yosei Ikeda photo
vastaction.com photo

RIDE UP A STEEP SLOPE

As always, stay on top of your pedals. As the slope steepens, gradually shift your body forward just enough to keep your feet heavy and your hands neutral.

- If you're pushing on the bars, you're too far forward.

- If you're pulling on the bars, you're too far back.

Moderately steep

You can stay in the saddle, but you have to pull your torso down and forward. This takes a lot of energy and still leaves your weight too far back.

You will hit every bump too rear-heavy. Your front end will get up easily and your rear will to try to stop you dead.

On any upslope, even small ones, it's best to use the below technique.

Very steep

Shift your hips forward and extend upward so you balance directly above the bottom bracket.

Most riders want to bend over while going up a hill like this. Encourage them to stand straight and use their bones, not their muscles, to maintain position. It's easier — and faster.

Master this technique! It helps with almost all upslopes, whether they're 10 inches or 10 feet tall. It also teaches balance.

Crazy steep

You reach a point where it's impossible to get far enough forward to be truly balanced on your feet.

Bend forward at the hips to get your head farther forward over the bars.

As you drive downward with your feet, pull backward with your hands. This multiplies force, which gives you more power and better rear traction.

Push and pull as hard as you can. But not so much the front end comes off the ground. It's a tricky balance.

RIDE DOWN A LEDGE

This fundamental technique works for ledges less than about 18 inches tall (which is pretty tall). It also helps riders stay balanced any time the trail dips downward.

Don't wait for your front wheel to pull you down — push it down!

Low attack position. The taller the ledge, the lower you have to get. Short stems help. General tip: The scarier the trail gets, the lower you have to be.

Push down aggressively as the front wheel starts to roll off.

Stay balanced on your feet the whole time. Light hands!

This drop is about 20 inches tall. The rider's head only dropped about six inches. A skilled rider can ride off a 18-inch ledge (or extend into an 18-inch backside) without drama.

Practice this skill on an ordinary curb. When riders can ride off with no head movement, increase the height. Make sure riders do this on every little trail drop.

If your head doesn't drop, the drop doesn't exist. By getting low and extending into trail depressions, you insulate your head from the terrain — and avoid those WHOA YIKES moments.

RIDE UP A LEDGE

Remember, it's all about staying balanced on your feet.

Get your front wheel up. This ledge is so steep it requires a powerful hip thrust while pulling your bars to your hips. If the rise is low or round enough, just roll up.

Shift your weight forward as your bike gets up onto the ledge (or water bar, or any sudden rise on the trail). This keeps your weight balanced on both wheels and lets your rear wheel roll smoothly over the ledge.

The crux move:
Drive hips forward as you pedal hard. Pull bars to hips. Stay above your pedals.

Neutral pedaling position

Neutral pedaling position

Neutral pedaling position

Do not lean back. When you do that, your front wheel clears easily but your rear wheel hits extra hard. If you're climbing slowly, you'll stop dead. If you're descending fast, you'll get bucked over the bars.

The A-1 key to riding up any ledge, rock, log, water bar or any other abrupt rise is ... drum roll please ... body position. Stay above your feet, and everything will be better.

PUMP SMOOTH BUMPS

BMX rollers and pump tracks are a great way to learn how to absorb (and pump) bumps. Put simply:

Stand in the low spots.

Crouch on the high spots.

Pull the bike up the frontsides. Each bump is a mini hill.

Push the bike down the backsides. Each bump is a mini drop.

Stay balanced over your feet* and generate power with your legs. Use your arms to match the bike angle to the bump angle.

*Advanced pump involves fore-aft movement, but that comes later.

1. Push down   **2.** Pull up   **3.** Stay centered!   **4.** Push down (mostly legs)

Get low   Stand tall

Get low! That is the A-1 key to pumping any bump. The lower you can get, the more pump you can get. These bumps happen to lead into and out of a bermed corner.

Yosei Ikeda photos

PUMP NATURAL TERRAIN

Yosei Ikeda photo

Once your riders learn to pump rollers, they can apply those principles on real terrain. Every bump — water bars, rocks, everything — becomes a feature to work. It's better to work the trail than to let it work you!

Even if your riders don't pump aggressively, their bikes should match the terrain angle and their heads and torsos should stay as level as possible. This will greatly increase control (and fun, and speed).

All rules of pump apply. See previous page.

Ignore the details. If a bump or ripple is less than four inches tall, it doesn't matter. Rather than focusing on the details of the terrain, see the overall shape. Where is it going up? Where is is going down? Get light on the ups, heavy on the downs.

The rougher the terrain, the more aggressive the rider has to be. Even if you're not trying to create speed, a committed pump will reduce impacts and increase control. Once you get in sync with a rough section, you must stay in sync. If you try to back out, you'll lose control.

Start slow and easy. Work your way up.

Anything with a backside can be pumped — even this block of sandstone. Unweight or hop over the front, then push down the back.

Pumping a natural roller

4. Extend fully for max pump

3. Push front end down backside

2. Bend low and absorb high spot

1. Extend legs into low spot

Heavy Loaded

Light Unloaded

Heavy Loaded

TROUBLESHOOTING

Problem: You feel your head and torso rocking back and forth through the bumps, even when you're going slow.

Solution: Make sure your hands are following the terrain. If a bump is 12 inches tall, your hands have to move at least 12 inches (the height of the bump plus the compression of your suspension).

Problem: Your head and torso are staying level, and everything feels smooth, but you still can't gain or maintain speed when you try to pump bumps.

Solution: Add some leg. Lee has taught hundreds of riders how to pump, and 90 percent of them have trouble controlling their legs like this. Make sure you're fully extended in the space between the bumps, and fully compressed (as low as you can get) on the tops of the bumps.

Problem: You keep hitting your seat.

Solution: Lower it. Even farther. If your bike's seat won't go low enough, consider a different seatpost. Remotely adjustable seatposts are awesome for trail riding.

Problem: Your low-speed pump feels good, but when you get going fast, you start hitting things and getting out of whack.

Solution: This is a good problem to have. As you go faster, you have to be more proactive. Pick up your front wheel before you reach the frontside, and push down the backside as hard as you can. This becomes a cycle: The harder you push, the earlier you can pull; the earlier you pull, the harder you can push.

Problem: You are a strong climber and a good all-around rider on your bike of choice, but you just can't seem to loosen up and rock the pump.

Solution: This is another common problem, especially among longtime XC riders. You need a change of venue. Get yourself a DJ hardtail or BMX cruiser. It will feel strange at first, but that strangeness might just open your body and mind to this whole new style of riding.

Problem: You feel like you're getting beaten to death on rough terrain.

Solutions: Make sure your bike is set up correctly. Shift your weight to your feet, loosen your grip, and relax your upper body. Look ahead. Load the bike in smooth sections and unload the bike in rough sections.

Problem: On rough terrain, you feel like you're balling up and getting stuck.

Solutions: Go faster. Unweight your bike, especially your front end, when you encounter obstacles.

Problem: When the going gets slick and loose, you feel like a sick goose.

Solution: This is pretty philosophical. When the ground sticks as well as a nonstick pan coated in cooking spray, you have to be willing to be out of control and go with it. That sounds pretty nutty, but that's the way it is. Wear pads if that helps your confidence. Like Steve Peat says: Expect your bike to slip. There, no more stress.

Problem: On loose ground, your front wheel digs in and pushes the dirt. Sometimes it catches and pitches you forward.

Solution: First, do not steer in loose dirt. Lean. Second, make sure your weight isn't too far forward. Start in your perfect attack position; then shift your weight a bit farther back.

Problem: On loose ground, your front wheel skims over the surface and refuses to steer.

Solution: Your weight is too far back. Move forward until your hands are neutral. To stick turns in loose ground, carefully press down on your bars.

Problem: You have trouble holding a line, whether it's between two ghastly ruts or across a narrow bridge.

Solution: Stay loose and look where you want to go (as always). Remember that a little momentum will carry you through a situation in less time than it takes to worry about that situation.

Problem: As you go down rough terrain, your bike feels like it won't move around. You feel like you're getting pitched forward. It's hard to lean into turns.

Solution: Your thighs might be interfering with the movement of your saddle. Spread your knees apart to let your bike bounce around and pitch into corners. Lower your seat!

Problem: You get beaten up while trying to pedal over rough terrain.

Solution: Get off the saddle, even if only a fraction of an inch. Put all your weight on your pedals and let your bike react to impacts. For lots of rough pedaling, lower your seat a quarter-inch or so to give yourself more room to work. For more powerful pedaling on relatively smooth sections, slide back on your saddle. This will approximate your normal height. Seriously consider a remotely adjustable seatpost.

DRILL - RIDING UP A RISE

What they'll learn

Balance for steep rises.

Why it's important

Every trail has myriad upslopes. Some are 12 inches tall and square-edged, and some are 12 feet tall and gradual, but they all use the same basic technique. This helps riders save energy and improve control on all rises.

Setup

Find an isolated rise that fits the level of your riders. Start smooth and mellow, and work up to steeper/more abrupt rises as riders improve. Suggestions:

Step 1: Smooth rise (6-10 feet tall) with moderate grade (~30%).

Step 2: Smooth rise with steep grade (~45%)

Step 3: Abrupt rise (a rock, water bar or ledge) about 12 inches tall.

How to run the drill

Coach explains the importance and reasons for shifting weight forward and maintaining balance on steep rises. Have riders ever had their front wheels come off the ground? Have they ever had their rear tires skid? Have they ever gotten their front wheel up something easily, then their rear hit and stopped them dead?

Coach holds a rider's bike on the rise and has the rider get on the bike and find a balanced position. Rider will be far forward. Make it clear this is the position — the only one — where the rider will be balanced. Riders must get that far forward.

Coach rides the rise and explains key points. Riders take their turns.

Watch for

Pulling hands. Sign that rider is too far back.

Pushing hands. Sign that rider is too far forward. Another sure sign: Rear tire skids.

Crouching low. Balance and power are improved when rider extends upward from pedals. Ask riders: Would you carry a TV like this (bend over) or like this (stand straight)?

Timing. Watch for riders adjusting their position before or after they hit the upslope. Riders should come forward *as* they hit the upslope. At every moment, they are balanced on their feet.

Whether rise is long or short, smooth or abrupt, as bike tilts upward, rider shifts forward to stay balanced over pedals.

DRILL - RIDING DOWN A DIP

What they'll learn

Balance for dips.

Why it's important

Every trail has myriad downslopes. Some are 12 inches tall and square-edged, and some are 12 feet tall and gradual, but they all use the same basic technique. This helps riders save energy and improve control on all dips.

Whether the dip is long or short, smooth or abrupt, as bike tilts downward, the rider shifts backward to stay balanced over pedals.

Setup

Find an isolated dip that fits the level of your riders. Start smooth and mellow, and work up to steeper/more abrupt rises as riders improve. You can use the same features as you did for going up rises.

Step 1: Smooth dip (6-10 feet tall) with moderate grade (~30%).

Step 2: Smooth dip with steep grade (~45%)

Step 3: Abrupt drop (a rock, water bar or ledge) about 12 inches tall.

How to run the drill

Coach explains the importance and reasons for shifting weight backward and maintaining balance on steep dips. Have the riders ever felt like they were riding their front wheels? Have they ever gone over the bars?

Coach holds a rider's bike on the dip and has the rider get on the bike and find a balanced position. Rider will be far backward. Make it clear this is the position — the only one — where the rider will be balanced. Riders must get that far backward or they'll be in trouble.

Coach rides the rise and explains key points. Riders take their turns.

Watch for

Pulling hands. Sign that rider is too far back. Rider will get pulled down the dip.

Pushing hands. Sign that rider is too far forward. Also trouble.

Head and torso getting pulled into the dip. Usually because rider came in too high and ran out of arm range. Riders must get low and extend into the dip. Ideally, torso stays level with horizon (in the middle photo at right, the slope is too steep and the stem is too long to allow a level torso).

DRILL - BASIC PUMP

What they'll learn

How to "pump" terrain: how to get light on frontsides and heavy on backsides.

Why it's important

Pump is the key to riding all terrain smoother and faster.

Setup

The place to learn pump is a series of several smooth 12- to 18-inch rollers. BMX tracks and pump tracks are ideal. Sections of trail can work.

How to run the drill

Different riders "get" pump in different ways. Run your group through the rollers repeatedly, focusing on the following points in this order. When each technique is introduced, the coach explains and demonstrates.

Focus on arms. Arms control the angle of the bike and ensure the rider is centered over the bottom bracket as the bike changes attitude. Actively pull the bike up the frontsides and push the bike down the backsides. Make sure riders bend their arms all the way on the peaks and extend all the way in the troughs. Tell them to try pulling themselves forward as they reach the top. This increases front-tire pump.

Try pumping on the front.

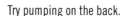

Focus on legs. Legs deliver most of the power. Once riders' arms are working, tell them to relax their hands and focus on their legs. For many riders this is much tougher. Get as low as possible on the peaks and extend fully in the troughs. Push HARD down the backsides and let the bike rebound up the frontsides. Keep the torso level. Tell riders to try leaning back on the backsides. This increases rear-tire pump.

Try pumping on the back.

Focus on being centered. Once the arms and legs are working independently, instruct riders to relax and ride the rollers as smoothly (and powerfully) as possible. Focus on heavy feet and light hands. Drive most of the power through the legs. Use the arms to *make* the bike go up on the ups and down on the downs. Centered pump is the safest and best way to handle most terrain.

Watch for

Find a perfect balance.

Arms and/or legs not using full travel.

Heads bobbing up and down.

Torsos rotating back and forward as riders go up and down rollers.

The more riders practice
core skills on training days,
the more they can relax and
rip on race days.

NICA photo

8

RIDE
WITH VISION

Goals:

- Make riders understand how their eyes work and how to best use them.

- Understand and practice visual reference points.

- Teach riders how to pick smart lines.

- Teach the skills and create the conditions for riders to find Flow (capital F).

YOUR EYES: THE RIGHT TOOLS FOR THE JOB

You can only ride as fast as you can see, and you can ride to places you've seen. Along with body position, vision is the A-1 most important riding skill — without good vision, you can't do any of the other skills!

Here are some tips to keep your eyes on:

Look ahead. This is so essential, but it's the first thing most riders forget, especially when they're stressed. Looking ahead improves your balance and reduces your perceived speed. Next time you're on the freeway, look at the ground right in front of your car — whoa, that's fast! — then scan ahead as far as you can see. Ahh, that's better.

Look where you want to go. Not where you don't want to go. We've all stared at that cliff edge or big rock and — whammo — we hit it every time. Notice bad spots on the trail, but immediately scan past them. You cannot ride where you haven't looked. If you want to keep moving, you must keep your eyes moving.

Pick targets. For trail riding, the most important targets are the entrances to turns (and the braking points just before them). Riding well is like a connect-the-dots puzzle. Pick your targets during training or race course inspection, and try to stay focused on them throughout your ride. The farther ahead your next target, the faster you can ride.

Soften your focus. A whole lot is happening in a mountain bike ride or race — the changing terrain, the other scheming riders — and you need to see it all. Rather than zero in on that root or the back of the leader's jersey, keep your eyes softly focused on your next target. This opens up your peripheral vision, which is designed to notice and track movement. You will see more of the trail and your competition.

Remember: The faster you can see, the faster you can ride.

Field of vision

Detailed vision is focused in a cone only 15 degrees wide. Let's call this "brain vision." It talks to the brain and is great for identifying targets and deciding where to go next.

The rest of a rider's vision is dedicated to tracking movement. Let's call this "body vision." It's talks more directly to the muscles and is ideal for mountain biking (and walking up stairs).

When a rider stares at the trail with brain vision, it slows down the body's reactions. When a rider relies on body vision, all movements are quicker and more fluid.

What this means: Riders should keep their brain vision scanning ahead for good targets, and let their body vision take care of everything else. Practice this with your team.

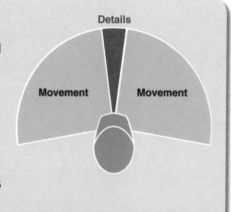

LOOK WHERE YOU WANT TO GO

This advice is easy to give but hard to follow. We all know riders should look as far ahead as possible, but what does that *mean*?

Practice choosing and using reference points on your training routes and race courses.

Look for: braking points, turning points, landmarks that set you up to be where you want to be.

As soon as you commit to Point A, look for point B. Examples:

Decide where you'll initiate your turn. Project yourself there.

This entire approach is designed to set you up for a wide turn entrance.

Rider is already thinking about the turn.

Start this turn. Find the next one.

Find a place to get heavy and redirect.

Committed to the redirection point. Scanning ahead to the next one.

These lines tend to be fastest in these types of corners.

Constant radius corner

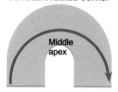

Increasing radius corner

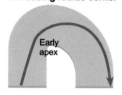

Decreasing radius corner

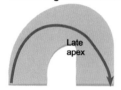

PICK SMART LINES

Line choice is perhaps the most complex aspect of mountain biking. You have to balance speed, equipment, skills, risk and your goals — all with your heart pounding and your eyeballs rattling. So where do you start?

If you're cruising or checking out a new trail, it's OK to follow the worn path.

If you're trying to ride your best — have the most fun or go the fastest — open your eyes and make some smart choices.

In general:

Set up for turns. Turns are most important. Go wherever you have to go to give yourself a good entrance.

　When in doubt: Use a late apex line. It's safest and often fastest.

Go as straight as possible. Trying to avoid bumps forces you to make extra turns, which can be slow and sketchy. Learn to trust your bike and body, and raise your threshold for obstacles that scare you. As you get more confident riding obstacles, go straigher and straighter over them.

Use the whole trail. The machines they use to build singletrack are four feet wide. The worn line is only one foot wide. Open your eyes. Set up extra wide for that turn. As world champion downhill racer Steve Peat says, "Don't be a sheep."*

It's all about the end. When you ride a trail section (or an entire trail), the only thing that matters is a clean exit out of the last corner. Everything you do before that corner should set you up for success in that corner.

*Remember, however, that it's not OK to ride off the built trail. Do not cut corners or create new trails to get the "better line" as this will increase erosion.

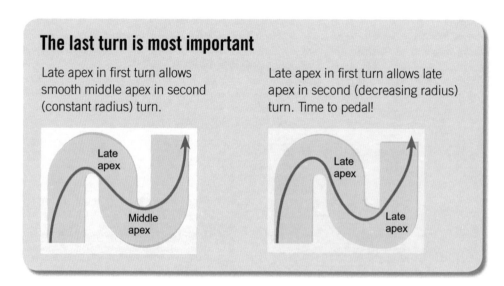

The last turn is most important

Late apex in first turn allows smooth middle apex in second (constant radius) turn.

Late apex in first turn allows late apex in second (decreasing radius) turn. Time to pedal!

Spend time with your team finding, discussing and riding smart lines.

Get low!

Extend your inside arm!

Enter tight turns as wide as you can, even if that puts you in the rocks.

Go as straight as you can. Strive for wide entrances.

Most riders go around the rocks, which is trickier and slower.

Looking into turn.

Setting up wide entrance.

Line choice is a skill. Practice it with your team.

FIND FLOW

Mountain biking satisfies so many desires. It transforms a gunnysack full of kittens into a ripped, hard body. It carries you through stunning places with exceptional people. Its sights, sounds, smells, and sensations block out all your inner demons. And, of course, the speed and magnitude of it all excite you like nothing else. You can go for half a dozen rides and enjoy them for half a dozen different reasons. Your lunchtime loop keeps you fit, Moab's Porcupine Rim Trail enthralls you, a twisty singletrack whips you like a roller coaster, a pump track keeps you strong and sharp.

These are all fantastic ways to enjoy our fine sport, but the ultimate experience happens when your thoughts crawl into your CamelBak and your body flows along the trail without effort or voice. Time changes. Tension disappears. You're focused but not forced. Controlling your bike becomes effortless. You've entered the magical state of "flow."

Dr. Mihaly Csikszentmihalyi describes the feeling of flow in his groundbreaking book, *Flow: The Psychology of Optimal Experience*: "Concentration is so intense that there is no attention left over to think about anything irrelevant, or to worry about problems. Self-consciousness disappears, and the sense of time becomes distorted. An activity that produces such experiences is so gratifying that people are willing to do it for its own sake, with little concern for what they will get out of it, even when it is difficult, or dangerous."

Does that sound familiar?

Flow only happens when the demands of the situation intersect with your abilities.

The trail isn't so hard that it scares you, nor is it so easy that it bores you. The further the demands lay above your perceived abilities, the bigger the rush. Savor a peaceful cruise down a local trail, enjoy a thrill behind a faster rider down a new path, or transcend all you thought possible by pinning it for an entire cross-country race. You might vomit at the end, but it feels so good, doesn't it?

We say "perceived" abilities because that's what counts. Most of us can climb harder, corner faster, and fly farther than we usually do. When you can let go of your inner mother and flow along in this zone, you'll have max fun and improve your riding.

Unfortunately, we can't just put on a Flow-Tron 2000 helmet and instantly feel that ecstasy. (If we could, we'd never do anything else.) According to the book Good Stress, Bad Stress by Barry Lenson (2002), flow is a precise psychological state that requires the elements described on the following page.

Fun happens where challenge meets skill

As a coach, its your job to make sure these elements apply to all your team rides.

Adequate skills. You don't learn to flow. You learn to ride your bike. When you can corner, hop, pump, and brake properly without thinking, then you can flow. You might achieve ecstasy in the soft Santa Cruz woods but flounder amid the raspy Phoenix boulders. When you worry about surviving the ride, you do not flow.

Goals. If you ride around—la, la, la—with no mission, you miss the rewards of accomplishing your goals. Set a goal. Spin smoothly, rail corners, stay on your buddy's wheel, or just stay on your bike for a change. If you need a ready-made structure, compete in a race. You have to know you're doing a good job.

Excitement. Too little stress and your mind wanders. Too much stress and you freak out. Go ahead and let some butterflies flutter in your tummy.

The good news is, achieving flow is neither random nor extremely difficult. Here are some tips to help you achieve flow more consistently and in crazier situations.

Break 'em down. Break big tasks into small components. For example: If you're trying to master a tricky turn, start by analyzing the ideal line, then looking through the turn, then leaning the bike, then turning your hips toward the next turn and finally pedaling out of the exit.

Practice. Don't just go out and ride, either. Pay close attention to what you're doing. Systematically build the skills you need to rip. Focus your mind on pedaling perfect circles. Then do a million of them.

Hang with the right crowd. Ride with people at or above your skill level. You will rise or fall to the level of your peers. Beware: If you feel inadequate around superior riders, or if they take you places you aren't ready for, you'll find it difficult to have a good time.

Pick the right tool for the job. You should not be worrying about your bike tracking correctly or holding together. Make sure your riders are on the right types of properly tuned bikes.

Conquer your obstacles. Pay attention to the things that prevent or interrupt your flow. Maybe you tense up every time you encounter baby head rocks. Either stay away from them or learn to ride them.

Don't pay attention to yourself. As soon as you realize you're ripping, the ripping pretty much stops. Remember that scene in The Empire Strikes Back when Luke stood on one hand with his eyes closed, with Yoda and a bunch of stuff balanced on his feet, and he started to levitate his X-wing fighter? He was definitely ripping. As soon as he opened his eyes and thought, "Yes! I'm a Jedi Master!" it all came crashing down. Don't be self-conscious like Luke Skywalker. Be confident like Han Solo and his partner Chewbacca!

TROUBLESHOOTING

Problem: As you zip along a trail, you get bogged down on certain obstacles; for example rocks, logs, or inflatable alligators.

Solutions: Practice similar obstacles in isolation. For example, if rocky ledges ball you up, hop the curb in front of your house 100 times a day. As always, keep your eyes moving. Notice the obstacle; then keep tracking forward.

Problem: While your buddies fly through technical sections, you get caught in all the tight corners.

Solution: Try following a straighter line over rocks and such. The less you have to turn, the better (assuming you can get over the rocks and such). When it's time to turn, get low and lean your bike!

Problem: You crash a lot.

Solution: Slow down and take mellower lines! Don't go fast and gnarly until you master slow and easy. If a certain trail or obstacle always messes you up, stop riding it! Take a step back, work on your skills, and then return.

Problem: You slow way down in rough sections where you can't pedal.

Solution: Pump the terrain. As an exercise, see how fast you can ride without pedaling. You'll be amazed at your high speed—and your high heart rate.

Problem: You get tense in certain situations, say, rock gardens or dense woods.

Solution: You're probably afraid for a reason—a crash, a scary clown, whatever. To ease your anxiety, ride these sections very slowly and strive for ultimate smoothness. Start increasing the speed after the scary clown leaves you alone. Remember to pump the terrain. Not only does it work better—but it also gives you something positive to focus on.